Date Due

Mr 6 '50	MAR 9	APR 26	APR 26
Mr 31 '50	FEB 18	FEB 10	MAY 21
N 6 '50	NOV 24	FEB 10	
N 10 '50	DEC 8	APR 5	
N 27 '50	DEC 12	JAN 17	
D 18 '50	OCT 8	APR 24	
F 15 '51	OCT 19	MAY 11	
Mr 6 '51			
N 21 '51	DEC 16	MAX 18	
D 5 '51	JAN 20	MAY 23	
MAR 20 '52	FEB 11		
FEB 9 '53	FEB 25		
APR 23 '53	MAR 9		
Wence	MAY 19		
Mar 25	MAR 5		
NOV 22	MAR 31		
FEB 11			
SEP 29			
MAY 8			

The City of the Seven Hills

*A Book of Stories from the History of
Ancient Rome*

BY

CAROLINE H. HARDING, A.B.

AND

SAMUEL B. HARDING, Ph.D.

ASSOCIATE PROFESSOR OF HISTORY IN INDIANA UNIVERSITY

Authors of "Greek Gods, Heroes and Men"

SCOTT, FORESMAN AND COMPANY

CHICAGO   ATLANTA   NEW YORK

PREFACE.

In this volume, the attempt has been made to give a picture of the life and history of the Roman people. So far as it has been feasible, this has been done by means of biographical sketches, selected so as to be illustrative of the Roman character, its virtues and its faults. In this way, it has also been possible to weave into the narrative a more vivid description of the daily life and customs of the men, women, and children of Rome, than would have been the case under any other method of treatment. In the last chapter, an attempt is made to relate the old Rome to modern life through a description of some existing remains, and to point out in a few words the way in which the ancient city was merged in the Rome of to-day.

In a work designed for young children, as is this one, it seems desirable that the brutal element of Roman character and history should be eliminated so far as is possible; and to this end, much has been omitted from the narrative which might properly find a place in a history of Rome for High School use. The limited view which is here offered, however, is a fundamen tally true one, and it may easily be developed into the accurate historical idea when the proper time comes for more advanced study.

The book is designed especially for use as a supplementary reader for children of the sixth and seventh grades. Inasmuch, however, as some teachers may wish to use it for formal instruction in history, the book has been equipped with maps, summaries of chapters, and a chronological analysis of Roman history. In this way, it is hoped that its use as a text-book may be facilitated without robbing it of its attractiveness as a reader.

BLOOMINGTON, INDIANA,
November, 1898.

TABLE OF CONTENTS.

LIST OF ILLUSTRATIONS.

The City of the Seven Hills.

I

The Peninsula of Italy.

IF you will look at the map of Europe you will see three great peninsulas extending from its southern coast into the Mediterranean Sea. The one farthest to the east is Greece, and upon the west, with the Atlantic washing its rocky shore, is Spain. Italy lies between the two, and it is with a people that lived and ruled there many centuries ago that these stories have to do.

As everyone must notice at the first glance these countries differ widely from one another in several ways. Greece is not nearly so large as Spain or Italy, and it has a number of smaller peninsulas running out from it into the surrounding seas. Spain is the largest of the three and is almost square in outline, with few bays or capes along its coast. Occupying a position between the others, Italy is also less extreme in size and shape. It is larger than Greece and smaller than Spain, and its coast line is neither so broken nor so regular as that of the one or the other. In form Italy is long and slender, being shaped very much like a

7

huge boot. On the map you will see it lying in the midst of the Mediterranean, its toe to the south and its heel to the east, and, with the island of Sicily, dividing the sea into two great basins.

Italy lies about as far north on the earth's surface as the State of New York, but it has a very different climate from that latitude in America. To the north of it is a high chain of mountains, which protects its sunny plains from the colder winds, while the sea about it is warmed by hot currents of air from the deserts of Africa. The winters are therefore milder and the summers warmer than with us, so that the orange and the olive grow in latitudes where our country produces only pears and apples.

The surface of Italy varies greatly in different parts of the peninsula. In the north between the steep wall of the Alps and the mountains to the south, lies a broad, well-watered plain larger than the State of Indiana. Here we find a most fertile land, with fields of grain and groves of waving mulberry trees. Here, too, is the largest stream of Italy, the River Po, which draws its waters from the melting snows of the Alps and flows eastward to the Adriatic Sea.

South of the basin of the Po we come again to a mountain range—the Apennines. These mountains are not so lofty as the Alps, but still are higher in many places than the tallest peaks of our Appalachians. From where they leave the Alps they sweep eastward almost across the country; then gradually curve to the south and extend to the end of the peninsula. Throughout the range many peaks are found covered to the top with forests of chestnut, oak, and pine

Pleasant valleys lie between the parallel ridges of the chain, and at the foot of the mountains are broad

uplands where flocks and herds find pasturage in the driest summer.

On the eastern side of this wooded mountain range

the slope is short, and the land is broken by deep gorges through which the rivers have cut their way to the Adriatic. Here only those can make their homes who live mostly on the products of their sheep and cattle. On the western slope the descent is more gentle, and broad, fertile plains lie between the mountains and the sea. The people do not have to depend so largely on their flocks here, for they can raise grain, and grow vineyards; and, in the south, groves of orange, fig, and olive trees may be seen.

As the peninsula is so narrow and the slope so abrupt, you could not expect to find long, deep rivers, in that part of the country which lies south of the River Po. Many streams rise in the mountains and flow down to the sea, but they are most of them short, and few are deep enough to bear a ship, or even a boat of large size. They vary, however, according to the season of the year. Sometimes, after the rains have begun to fall, or when the snow is melting on the tops of the mountains, they are rushing torrents which sweep everything before them. Then, again, when the summer heats have come, and the rains have ceased, they shrink to little, harmless streams, or dry away altogether. The only river, south of the valley of the Po, which is deep enough to bear boats and small ships throughout the year is the Tiber; but even this changes with the seasons. It has been called "the yellow Tiber," because its swift current is so often colored with floods from heavy rains and melting snows upon the mountain sides.

With such a marked difference between the eastern and western slopes of Italy it would not be difficult to guess where the first cities were built. From early times the western side was dotted with little towns, some of them so well located that people have been content to go on building and living in them for more than twenty centuries. There were also ancient cities on the shores of the wide plain that borders the gulf on the south. But in those days, as now, there were few towns on the rocky eastern coast; and even to the north, upon the low sandy islands at the mouth of the Po, where Venice now stands, there were then only the homes of a few scattered fishermen.

As you know, Italy is now the seat of a nation united under the government of one king. But at the time to which the first stories of the country go back, about seven hundred and fifty years before Christ, there was no kingdom of Italy and no Italian nation. Then there were only separate groups of people established here and there, those nearest together being distantly related perhaps, but having very little to do with each other in spite of that. They knew much less about their country than we do now, for there were no books then to tell them about it, and in every direction the mountains, the rivers, or the sea hemmed them in, and made traveling so difficult that they could not well see it for themselves. So it happened that most of these peoples were acquainted only with the groups that lived close by them; and they were interested only in their own little city, with their farms and pasture-lands about it. It would not have been possible at that time to have had one ruler for the whole peninsula as there is now. Instead, each little town had its own king, who governed his people in time of peace and led them in war, when they fought against their neighbors.

These cities were always built on a hill or in some high situation that could easily be defended against their enemies. There they placed their fort, or citadel, and the rest of the town would cluster about it. The people would go out into the surrounding country to cultivate their farms and tend their cattle, but to this spot they always retreated in time of danger. Every town lived more or less to itself, obeying its own king, fighting its own battles, and controlling a few miles of land about it.

In very early times such a city lay on the south bank of the Tiber, about twenty miles from the sea. It was called Rome, and at first was probably not very different from many other towns in Italy. As time went on, however, it became much greater than its neighbors. It conquered first the cities that lay nearest to it, then those farther and farther away until it had made the whole of Italy its own. After this it reached out and conquered all the countries about the Mediterranean, and, in a certain sense, became what it has often been called, "the Mistress of the World."

II

Romulus and the Beginning of Rome.

WE do not know just when, or how, or by whom the beginning of Rome was made. It happened so long ago, and there was so little writing in those early days, that no account, given at the time, has come down to us. Indeed, it is likely that nobody then dreamed that the world would ever care to know how this little city was commenced.

But, after Rome had begun to grow, and to conquer her neighbors, and people had begun to read and write, the Romans themselves began to be curious to know about the beginning of their town. It was too late to find out certainly then, for the persons who had lived at the time that it was founded were long dead and forgotten. But the Romans continued to wonder about it, and finally they made up many stories of the early years of their city, which they came to accept as true and have handed down to us.

According to these stories, the first settlers at Rome came from a little city named Alba Longa, and this was the way in which they happened to leave that place and settle at Rome. The rightful king of Alba Longa had been put out of power by his brother. Then this brother had killed the true king's sons, and shut up his daughter in prison, where twin sons were born to her. When her cruel uncle heard this, and saw how large and strong the children were, he was much troubled; for he feared that, if they should grow up to be men, they might some day take his stolen throne away from him. He determined, therefore, to put them to death; so he took the sleeping children in the wooden trough which served as their cradle, and gave them to a servant, telling him to drown them in the River Tiber.

The river at this time was overflowing its banks, and the main current ran so swift and strong that the man was afraid to go near the bed of the stream. For this reason, he set the trough down in the shallow water at the river's edge, and went his way. The children floated gently in this strange boat to a place where seven low hills rose upon the southern bank of the stream. The flood was now going down rapidly; and at the foot of a wild fig tree, which grew at the base of one of these hills, the cradle at last caught in a vine and came safely to land.

In this way the children escaped drowning, but they were still alone and uncared for, far from the homes of men. Soon, however, they were provided for in a wonderful manner. When they began to cry of hunger, a mother wolf that had lost her cubs came to them, and gave them milk, and a woodpecker flew down from the trees bringing them food. For some time these wild creatures were the children's only nurses, but at last a shepherd of Alba Longa, who had often watched the wolf coming and going from the place, found the boys and saw how they had been cared for. The Italians of that time thought that wolves and woodpeckers were sacred to Mars, their god of war; so this shepherd believed that the children were favorites of that deity. Full of this thought, he carried them to his little hut, where his wife took charge of them as though they had been her own.

The children were named Romulus and Remus by the shepherd people, and as the years passed they grew up strong and brave, with spirits that nothing could subdue. Whenever there was a hunting party, or a contest in running or wrestling, or a struggle with robbers who tried to drive off their flocks and herds, Romulus and Remus were sure to be among the leaders of the shepherd band.

They won great fame among their companions, but they also gained the hatred of evil-doers. At last, some lawless men, in revenge, seized Remus at a festival, and bore him to the false king of Alba Longa, charging him with robbery. There the true king saw the young man, and, struck with his appearance, questioned him about his birth; but Remus could tell him little. In the meantime, the shepherd who had found the boys told Romulus the whole story of the discovery of Remus and himself; and Romulus gathered together a company of his friends, and hurried to the city to save his brother. In this he soon succeeded; and then the two brothers joined together to punish the cruel king of Alba Longa, and to set their newly-found grandfather on his throne once more.

After they had accomplished this the brothers were not content to remain in Alba Longa, for they wished to be rulers wherever they might be. As there were now more people in Alba than could live comfortably within its walls, it was decided to begin a new city under the leadership of Romulus and Remus; and the two brothers chose a location near the fig tree where they had been found as children by their foster-father.

This was an excellent place for a city. On the nearest hill, which was called the Palatine, they could build their fort; and at its foot were valleys in which they could pasture their sheep and cattle. The River Tiber was near at hand, for their rude boats to come and go upon; and if, at any time, the city should grow too large for this one small hill, there were the six others close by to receive the overflow of people.

After Romulus and Remus had decided upon the place for their town, a difficulty arose. A new city must have a founder who should give his name to it; but which of the brothers should have this honor? As they were of the same age, and could not settle the matter by giving the honor to the elder, they agreed to leave the choice to the gods of the place. So each took his stand upon one of the hills to receive a sign by watching the flight of birds. Remus saw six vultures from his hill-top; but Romulus, a little later, saw twelve. This was thought to be a better sign than that of Remus; so Romulus became the founder of the new city, and it was called Rome after him.

The new ruler first marked off the boundaries of the city by hitching cattle to a plough and drawing a deep furrow around the hill. After this had been done they raised a wall about the place and Romulus invited to his new town all who might wish to come and settle there. He soon had a strong company of men about him, for many of his rude shepherd friends and many of the youths of Alba joined him. Then as the report of the new town spread among the neighboring cities, men from other places, slaves as well as freemen, joined him from time to time.

But though the little city was growing sturdily there was one thing that was still lacking. Among all the men that came flocking into Rome there were few, if any, women. So the town was more like a camp of soldiers than a city of homes and families founded to endure for years. The men felt this want so keenly that at last they seized some of the women of the neighboring tribe of the Sabines and bore them into Rome to be their wives.

Of course this bold deed startled and alarmed the people around them, and the Romans soon found that they must fight to keep the wives they had taken by force. The powerful Sabine tribe came marching against the city, with their king at their head. First a fort which had been built on a hill called the Capitol fell into their hands. Then, on the next day, the Romans and the Sabines met in battle in the valley between the Capitol and the town. For a long time the fight raged fiercely; first one army and then the other seemed victorious, but neither the Romans nor the Sabines would own themselves defeated.

At last, the captive Sabine women took courage to interfere and stop the bloodshed. They threw themselves between the weapons of their relatives on the one side, and of their newly-made husbands on the other; and they implored them to stop the fight, as it must bring sorrow to them, no matter who became the victors. Then the battle ceased, and the leaders of the Sabines, moved by the appeal of the women, came forward to make peace. It was agreed that the Romans should keep their wives, and that the Sabines should go to Rome to live, where the two peoples were to share the city between them.

From this time the new town grew rapidly, and it soon spread to others of the seven hills by the Tiber. Its citizens became so strong in war that none of their neighbors could harm them. In war and in peace, Romulus was their leader, and was greatly beloved by the people. According to the old stories, he made many laws for them and established many good customs. He ordered that every eighth day there should be a market held in Rome, at which the country folk might sell their produce; and he himself heard cases and dealt out justice there in the market place. To aid him in the government, he formed an assembly of the older and wiser men, which was called the Senate, or the council of the city fathers.

Thus Romulus ruled his people for thirty-seven years. Then, one day, as he was reviewing the army, a sudden darkness fell upon the earth, and a mighty storm of thunder and lightning came upon them. When this had passed, and the air was clear once more, Romulus could nowhere be seen. While the Romans were seeking their king, and mourning for him, a citizen came forward, who said that, in the midst of the storm, he had seen Romulus carried up to heaven in the chariot of the war-god, Mars. After that the people ceased to mourn for him, for they believed that he had become a god; and from that time on they not only honored him as the founder of their city, but worshiped him as one of the deities of heaven.

III

Numa, the Peaceful King.

AFTER Romulus had been taken from them, the Romans could not agree as to who should be king in his place. The citizens who had first settled there wished to choose a king from their own number again, but the Sabines objected to this. They said that they had faithfully obeyed Romulus while he lived, and that now it was their turn to have a king chosen from among themselves.

For a time the two parties could not come to an agreement, and, while they were disputing, the Senate took the power of king and carried on the government. This, however, did not please the people. They said that now they had many kings, instead of one, and they demanded that a real monarch should be chosen. At last, it was arranged that the first citizens should select a ruler from among the Sabines, and Numa was then chosen to fill the place of Romulus.

The new ruler was different from the old one in many ways. The first king had been a great soldier, and he had trained the people of the city for war; but during his reign the men of Rome had little time or thought to give to anything else. King Numa was convinced that this was not as it should be—that there were other things of more importance than the knowledge of war and the art of winning battles. He felt that the Romans were too harsh and violent, as warlike people always are; and he wished to soften their manners and make them less rude in thought and deed. He made peace with all the enemies of Rome; and, during the forty-three years of his reign, there was no war. This left the Romans free to till their fields, and learn the arts of peace; and to encourage them in this, Numa divided among the citizens the lands which Romulus had won in battle.

Numa ruled his people as a wise and peaceful king; but, better than this, he also taught the Romans how to honor their gods. The Romans believed in many gods; almost every thing, and every act, was thought by them to be under the control of some deity. In later times, when they came to know the Greeks, they confused their own gods with those of their new acquaintances; and even after this they adopted gods of other peoples with whom they came in contact. So if you tried to know all the deities that the Romans believed in, you would have to learn a long and uninteresting list. But there were a few that held a very important place in the life of the people from the first, and the worship of these was thought to have been established during the reign of Numa.

The chief of the gods was Jupiter—or Jove—the Sky-father, whom they called the "Best" and "Greatest." He sent forth the clouds and ruled the storm, and the thunderbolt was his weapon. The Romans thought that he directed the birds whose flight showed the will of the gods to men, and that Victory and Good Faith were his constant attendants.

Next to the great Jupiter the fierce Romans worshiped their god of battles, the warlike Mars. Strangely enough, Mars was also the god who preserved their cattle from disease, and their ripening grain from

JUPITER

blight and injury. The goddess Juno, as the wife of Jupiter, was the queen of the sky. It was she, they thought, who cared especially for the Roman women and made their children strong and vigorous. Minerva was the goddess of wisdom and inventions. She taught men the use of numbers, and each year a priest solemnly drove a nail into the temple to keep count of the passing years. On her festival the children had a holiday, for she was the goddess of schools and of all learning. Vesta was the goddess of the fire upon the hearthstone, and was worshiped wherever a Roman family made its home.

Last of all, there was a curious god of Beginnings, called Janus, whose favor the Romans begged whenever they began anything new. The first month of the year was called in his honor "January," or the month of Janus. He was especially the god of gateways; and when the Romans wished to represent him, they made a figure with two faces, to show that, as guardian of the gate, Janus must look in both directions. When the Romans were at war with any people the gates of his temple stood open, but they were closed in time of peace. During the reign of Numa, therefore, they were fast shut, and this was often recalled by the Romans in later times, when grown men could not remember ever having seen that gateway closed.

The Romans already believed in these gods when Numa became king, but he showed them more exactly how each should be worshiped. He seemed so wise in these sacred matters that the Romans came to think that he must have been taught by one of the gods themselves. It was whispered that he was often seen wandering forth to a grove where dwelt a mountain spirit, the nymph Egeria, and the people at last believed that this spirit loved him and instructed him as to what would be pleasing to each of the immortal gods.

One of the things that Numa did was to divide the priests into different companies and to give each its own share in the worship of the deities. In this way, he set apart separate priests for Jove and Mars and Romulus; and the chiefs of these priests, together with the king, were the high priests of Rome, and had charge of all things connected with religion. A company of sacred heralds was also formed, whose business it should be to make a solemn declaration of war when the Romans took up arms against an enemy, and to proclaim the treaty of peace when the war was at an end.

There was one of these groups of priests which arose in a peculiar way, and had very curious duties. These were the "dancing priests" of Mars, and the Roman writers say that they dated from the eighth year of the reign of Numa. Then a great sickness came upon the Romans; and while the people were much disheartened on this account, suddenly a shield of brass fell from the heavens at the feet of King Numa. When he consulted the nymph Egeria concerning it, she told him that it was the shield of Mars, which the god had sent down for the preservation of the people; and that it should be kept with the greatest care.

In order to do this King Numa commanded that eleven other shields just like this one should be made, so that, if an enemy of the Roman people should attempt to steal the shield of Mars, he might not be able to tell the true one from the false. Then the king appointed twelve young men of the noblest families to take the shields in charge, and he arranged a yearly

festival which they should keep in honor of the pre·
server of their city.

Each year, when March—the month of Mars—came,
these priests were to take the sacred shields, and go
leaping and dancing through the streets of the city,
singing old songs in honor of the god. This festival
lasted for twenty-four days, and each day the procession came to an end at some appointed place. Here
the shields were taken into one of the houses near by,
and the dancing priests were entertained with a fine
supper.

Numa also ordered that whenever a war should break
out, and it became necessary for a Roman army to
march to battle, the general should first go to the altar
of the war-god, and strike the sacred shields, crying:

"Awake, Mars, and watch over us!"

Then—so the Romans believed—the god would
answer their appeal by marching unseen before the
army as it went forth to battle. In later days stories
were told of threatened defeat, when the god had
appeared in the form of a valiant young man, encouraging and strengthening the soldiers, and leading them
on at last to victory.

The priestesses of Vesta, the goddess of the hearth
fire and the home, were as important as these priests
of Mars. For the worship of this goddess Numa
formed a company of six young maidens, chosen from
the noblest families of Rome. It was their duty to
offer prayers each day in the circular temple of the
goddess, and, above all, to see that the sacred fire
which burned upon Vesta's altar, was never allowed
to die out.

These maidens were called the Vestal Virgins, and they entered into the service of the goddess in their early childhood.   Little girls between the ages of six and ten were always selected, and as each one was appointed to this great honor she was taken from her father's house to the house of the Vestals, where she was to live for thirty years.   The first ten years she spent in learning the duties of her office.   During the next ten she practiced what she had learned, and for the last ten she taught the newly-made Vestals their sacred duties.   When the thirty years were past, she might leave the Vestals and have a home of her own, if she chose; but she rarely did so.   Great honor was shown her by the Romans, and she was allowed to bestow unusual favors; for instance, if a criminal chanced to meet a Vestal Virgin on his way to imprisonment, he was at once set free.

In these various ways Numa was thought to have arranged the service of the different gods.   By the religious dances and the processions that he appointed, he made their worship attractive to the Romans. They followed faithfully the customs that he had established for them with so much thought and care, and in the course of time they began to lose some of the fierceness that had marked the first rude settlers.   But this did not come to pass until long after King Numa had died peacefully, so honored by all the nations about Rome that they sent crowns and offerings to his funeral.

IV

The Last of the Kings.

AFTER the death of Numa, the long peace which Rome had enjoyed came to an end. Under the kings who followed him, the wars with her neighbors were renewed, and it was centuries before the gates of the temple of Janus again stood closed. These rulers were all good warriors, so that the Romans were usually successful in their battles, and their lands were increased, bit by bit, through their conquests. But, above all, the Romans learned two valuable lessons in these times. They learned to fight bravely and well; and to obey their rulers in war and in peace.

After a number of years, trouble arose between Rome and Alba Longa, its mother city. War followed, and the men of Alba were defeated. Then it was agreed that the people of that town should leave their homes and seek new ones at Rome; and the city of Alba Longa was destroyed.

These settlers from Alba were so numerous that the population of Rome was nearly doubled by their coming. As the city grew, the hills about the Palatine were occupied, one after the other, and Rome could then truly be called "the City of the Seven Hills." It became necessary to defend these later parts, also, and new walls of stone were built which included all of the seven hills. So large was the space which they inclosed, that for many hundreds of years the city did not outgrow them; and so well were they built, that parts of them are still standing to this day.

The next step after defending the greater city was to improve it. The valleys which lay between the

hills were low and consequently marshy in places. To drain these and make them healthful for men to dwell in, great sewers were built which emptied their waters into the River Tiber. In one of the valleys, also, a course was laid out for the chariot races, of which the Romans were very fond.

On the hill called the Capitol, a great temple was built in honor of the three gods, Jupiter, Juno, and Minerva. This was planned upon such a large scale that it covered eight acres of ground, and remained the chief center of Roman worship until it was burned five hundred years later. Its gates were of brass, covered with gold; while the inside was of marble and was decorated with gold and silver ornaments. When the workmen were laying its foundations, they had to remove a number of altars that had already been set up there; but the altar of the god of Youth, and that of the god of Boundaries, they found could not be moved. Then the priests declared this a sign that Rome should ever remain young and strong, and that her boundaries should never be moved backward. So the two altars remained where they had long stood, and the workmen carefully inclosed them in the new temple, firm in the belief that the prophecy concerning their city would be fulfilled.

While this great temple was still unfinished, an old woman came one day to the king of Rome. She brought with her nine rolls of paper,—"books" the Romans called them, though they were quite unlike what we know as such. In these rolls were written many oracles and prophecies that told how the wrath of the gods might be turned away whenever it had brought sickness, famine, or other misfortune upon the people. She offered to sell the books to the king, but the price she asked seemed so high that he refused to buy them.

At this the old woman went away and burned three of the books. Then she returned and offered the king the six that remained, but she demanded for them the price which she had before asked for the nine. Again he refused to buy. Once more the old woman burned three of the books, and came back offering the king the ones that were left for the price that she had at first asked for all.

Conquered by her persistence, the king at last yielded. He bought the three remaining books for what she asked; and when the temple on the Capitol was finished, they were placed in a vault under it for safe keeping. After this, whenever any trouble came upon the city, one of the first things that the Romans did was to consult these books; and the message which the priests found in them, the people accepted as the voice of the gods.

After many years, the seventh king sat on the throne of Rome, and men called him Tarquin the Proud. He was a cruel and wicked man, very different from the earliest kings. He had gained his power by bloodshed and violence, and he used it like a tyrant. He repealed the good laws which had been made under the rulers before him, and made others in their place. The nobles complained that he did everything according to his own will, and never asked the Senate for its advice and assistance. The people, in their turn, murmured at the constant wars which he carried on, and the hard tasks at which he set them in time of peace. At last, all Rome was weary of his rule, and the people of the city only needed some one to direct them in order to turn against him.

They found their leader in a noble named Brutus, who had suffered much at the hands of the king. His brother had been put to death by Tarquin; and Brutus, to save himself from a like fate, had been obliged to give up his property and seem to be dull and slow of mind, so that the king might find nothing in him to fear.

But beneath this mask of stupidity the real Bru was keen and watchful. Once he had been sen the companion of the king's sons when they wen consult the great Oracle at Delphi, in Greece. A finishing the business upon which they had gone, young men asked the Oracle which one of them shou succeed King Tarquin as ruler of Rome. The Oracl replied, that he who first kissed his mother upon their return should rule the city. The princes hastened to draw lots to decide which one of them should have that privilege, and so gain the throne, but Brutus understood the prophecy better. He pretended to stumble and fall, kissing the ground beneath him as he did so, for he guessed that the Oracle had not meant a person, but the great Earth, the mother of them all.

In spite of the discontent among the citizens, Tarquin might, perhaps, have been king of Rome until he died, if it had not been for the great wickedness of one of his sons. While the king was away from the city, carrying on war with a neighboring people, this son, Sextus, caused the death of a noble Roman lady named Lucretia. Her husband and her father were overcome with grief and rage, and Brutus, who was with them, threw off his pretended dulness. He seized the bloody dagger that had slain Lucretia, and swore with them that he would never rest until the family of

Tarquin had ceased to reign at Rome. Then he hurried to the city and told the story there. The people were filled with anger, and when the king and his sons returned, they found the gates closed against them. Their soldiers had already received Brutus with joy, and, having lost both army and city, the king was obliged to leave the lands of Rome and seek refuge among his friends north of the Tiber.

After they had cast out the Tarquins, the people took an oath that they would never, from that time on, allow any one to become king in Rome. Then one of the first things which they had to do was to find some other form of government to take the place of the old one. For they knew very well that they must have some one in authority over them, or their enemies would be able to overcome their army, and King Tarquin might seize his throne once more.

So the people set up a republic. They agreed that two men, called consuls, should be elected each year; and these consuls, with the Senate, should govern Rome in the place of the kings. When the vote was taken for the first consuls, it was found that Brutus was one of the two men who were elected; so the oracle was fulfilled which foretold that he should follow Tarquin as ruler of the city.

V

The War with Lars Porsena.

TARQUIN THE PROUD was not content, however, to see his kingdom slip from him so easily; and the Roman people were soon obliged to fight for the right of governing themselves. Their first trouble came from within the city itself; and this, perhaps, no one had expected.

There were some of the people of Rome who were not pleased at the expulsion of the king, and who would have been glad to have him back with them again. These persons were young men of high family and much wealth, who had been the companions of the young princes, and who had enjoyed rights and privileges under the rule of Tarquin, which were now taken away from them. They complained bitterly of this, and said that, though the rest of the people had gained by having the Tarquins go, they had lost by it. So, when the opportunity offered itself, they began working selfishly to return the king to power.

Their chance came when Tarquin sent men back to Rome to claim the property which he and his sons had left behind them, when they had been driven away. While these men were in the city, they made a plot with the dissatisfied young nobles to place King Tarquin on his throne once more. This was treason on the part of the young nobles; but they cared more for their own pleasures than they did for their country. However, the plot was discovered by a slave, and from

LICTORS.

him the consuls learned of it. When the plotters had been seized, it was found that among them were the two sons of the consul Brutus himself.

It was part of the duty of a consul to act as judge in the trial of prisoners, and this made the situation doubly terrible for Brutus. But he was a true Roman, and loved his country even more than he did his own children. He took his seat with the other consul, and, when the young men were led before the judges, he joined in condemning them all to death. Then the prisoners were given into charge of attendants of the consuls, called lictors, who each carried a battle-ax, bound into a bundle of rods, as a sign that the consuls had the right to punish offenders with flogging and with death itself. They made the erring young nobles suffer the full severity of the law, and the Romans saw, with admiration and pity, that the stern virtue of Brutus did not fail him even when the welfare of his country demanded that his sons be put to death before his eyes.

Tarquin was only made more angry and determined by the failure of this plot. He now decided that if he could not get back his throne by treachery, he would try to do so by open war. He went about from city to city, begging help from the enemies of Rome to bring his people back under his rule once more. No matter how often he was refused, or how often he was defeated in battle when he did succeed in raising a force to lead against the Romans, he was always ready to try again.

At last Tarquin secured the help of Lars Porsena, who ruled over a part of Tuscany, as the district is called which lies north and west of the Tiber. The story of the attack which followed was cherished as long as there was a Roman people to glory in the

'leeds of its heroes, and even within our time an
English writer chose it for the subject of a stirring
poem.* In this you may read how

> Lars Porsena of Clusium,
>   By the Nine Gods he swore
> That the great house of Tarquin
>   Should suffer wrong no more.
> By the Nine Gods he swore it,
>   And named a trysting day,
> And bade his messengers ride forth,
> East and west and south and north,
>   To summon his array.

When the Romans heard this news, they were filled
with dismay; and from all sides the country people
flocked into the city. Never before had so great a
danger threatened the place. The Senate and consuls
prepared as well as they could to meet the attack, and
tried to hope that they might still be able to defeat
their enemies.

Just across the river from Rome was a long, high
hill. Here the Romans had built a fort as a protection to the city; and to connect this with Rome, a
wooden bridge had long ago been placed across the
rapid current of the Tiber. If the Romans could hold
this height and the bridge below it the city would be
safe. But by a quick march and fierce attack Lars
Porsena and the Tarquins seized the hill. Then their
soldiers pushed on to gain the bridge also, while many
of the Romans who guarded it were struck with fear
and turned to take refuge in the city.

---

* See Macaulay's *Lays of Ancient Rome.*

At this moment a Roman named Horatius rushed in among his countrymen, laying hold of them, and standing in the way of their flight.

"Why do you flee?" he cried. "If you give up the bridge there will soon be more of the enemy in Rome than here. Break down the timbers with fire and sword before you go! I will guard the entrance for you as well as one man may."

At these words the soldiers were seized with shame. Two of their number stepped to Horatius's side to defend the narrow entrance with him, and the others fell to work tearing down the bridge behind them. Until the last beams were ready to fall Horatius and his comrades stood at the end, holding all the army of Lars Porsena in check upon the other side. Though many tried to overcome them, no man proved himself a match for them. Wounded but unflinching, they fought until the bridge began to tremble, and the laboring soldiers warned them to return while there was still a way. At the call Horatius's companions fell back, step by step, but their leader lingered, fighting to the last. Then just as he had turned to cross, with a mighty crash the bridge fell; and he was left, cut off among his enemies.

> Alone stood brave Horatius,
>   But constant still in mind;
> Thrice thirty thousand foes before,
>   And the broad flood behind.
> "Down with him!" cried false Sextus.
>   With a smile on his pale face.
> "Now yield thee," cried Lars Porsena;
>   "Now yield thee to our grace."

Round turned he, as not deigning
   Those craven ranks to see;
Naught spake he to Lars Porsena,
   To Sextus naught spake he;
But he saw on Palatinus
   The white porch of his home;
And he spake to the noble river
   That rolls by the towers of Rome.

"O Tiber! Father Tiber!
   To whom the Romans pray,
A Roman's life, a Roman's arms,
   Take thou in charge this day."
So he spake, and speaking sheathed
   The good sword by his side,
And with his harness on his back,
   Plunged headlong in the tide.

No sound of joy or sorrow
   Was heard from either bank;
But friends and foes in dumb surprise
With parted lips and straining eyes,
   Stood gazing where he sank;
And when above the surges
   They saw his crest appear,
All Rome sent forth a rapturous cry,
And even the ranks of Tuscany
   Could scarce forbear to cheer.

But Horatius was weary and wounded from the fight, and his armor weighed heavily upon him. Many times he seemed sinking in midstream, but each time he rose again. At last, he felt the bottom under his feet and safely climbed the other shore.

The city was saved, and mainly by Horatius. The state was grateful to him for his brave deed, and the Senate ordered that he should have as much of the public land as he could plough around in one day. Later his statue was set up in the Forum, but best of all was the gratitude which the people showed him at the time. Then, when food became scarce because of the war with Lars Porsena, the citizens each brought to the house of Horatius little gifts of grain and wine, so that whatever suffering might come upon themselves, there would still be plenty in the house of the man who had saved Rome. And long afterwards we can imagine the people relating the story.

> When the goodman mends his armor,
>   And trims his helmet's plume;
> When the goodwife's shuttle merrily
>   Goes flashing through the loom;
> With weeping and with laughter
>   Still is the story told,
> How well Horatius kept the bridge
>   In the brave days of old.

VI

The Stories of Mucius and Clœlia.

AFTER Lars Porsena had failed in his attempt to seize the bridge over the Tiber his army lay for a long time about Rome. He pitched his camp on the plains before the walls, and sent in all directions for boats to guard the river so that no provisions could enter the city. Then companies of his men scattered through the Roman territory, plundering and destroying as they went.

The Romans were thus kept closely inside their walls, and with them the people from the surrounding country who had found shelter there. Porsena and the Tarquins rejoiced, for they knew that there would soon be a lack of food with so many to consume the Roman stores; and sure enough, as the blockade continued, corn became scarce and very high in price. Still the imprisoned army could not venture forth to battle without risking certain defeat against such great numbers. The most that was attempted by Rome was to capture a band of pillagers, and so put a stop to their wandering over the country. This forced inaction at a time of such great need seemed disgraceful to the Roman youths, and they longed, at whatever cost, to be again contending with their enemies.

Lars Porsena was expecting nothing but complete victory, when something occurred that daunted him and changed his purpose. A young Roman was seized in his camp, who had dared to come thither to fight his enemies single-handed, since he was not allowed to do so with his comrades upon the field of battle. When he was brought before Porsena he did not hesitate to declare his purpose.

"I am a Roman citizen. My name is Caius Mucius. An enemy, I wish to slay an enemy, nor have I less resolution to suffer death than to inflict it. To act and to suffer with fortitude is a Roman's part. Therefore, if you choose to remain here, prepare yourself for this peril,—to contend for your life every hour, to have the sword and the enemy at the very entrance to your tent. This is the war that we, the Roman youth, declare against you."

Then, when the startled king demanded to know more of the danger that threatened him, and ordered fires to be kindled about the young man if he did not explain his words more fully, Mucius only replied:

"Behold, and see of how little account the body is to those who have great ends in view!" As he spoke he thrust his hand into the fire which was burning upon an altar near by, and held it there without sign of pain or flinching.

Astonished at this act the king arose from his throne and commanded that the young man be removed from the altar.

"You have acted more like an enemy to yourself than to me," he said, "I should encourage you to be always so brave, if your valor were only shown upon the side of my country. I now dismiss you untouched and unhurt."

As though making a return for this kindness, Mucius answered:

"Since courage is so honored by you, O King, I will tell you that three hundred of the best of the Roman youths have vowed to come after me, each in his turn."

When Porsena heard this, he realized how hard it would be to take Rome if its people were willing to give up their lives so unselfishly for their city. He sent Mucius back in safety, and offered to make peace of his own accord. He agreed to take his army away from around the walls of the town, but he demanded pledges that the Romans would keep the peace. They gave him sons and daughters from the noblest families, and he took them away with him as hostages, so that they might have to fear the punishment of their children if they were tempted to break their promises.

Among the hostages who were obliged to go with Lars Porsena was a high-spirited girl named Clœlia. She did not like to live as a captive in a strange camp, and she made a plan to escape. Porsena's army then lay not very far from the city, on the banks of the Tiber; and one day Clœlia, taking a number of other girls with her, managed to swim across the river, and reached Rome in safety.

When the king was told of the escape of the hostages, he was very angry, and sent messengers to demand that Clœlia and her companions should be returned to him. The Romans kept their faith, and sent the girls back to Porsena; for they thought that they had no right to keep the children simply because they had escaped so bravely. When Porsena saw that the Romans were acting fairly in the matter, his anger died away, and he became as generous as they had been just. He led all the Roman prisoners before Clœlia, and bade her choose half of them to return with her to their homes. She selected the youngest of the band and was sent back to the city with them in great honor, for both the Romans and their enemies united in praising her strength and courage. When the war was over the city placed her statue, mounted upon a horse, at the top of the Sacred Way,—an unusual honor for a woman, called forth by an uncommon act of bravery.

Even after Lars Porsena had made peace with the Romans, Tarquin was not satisfied that he would never again be allowed to rule at Rome. When he found that Porsena would no longer help him, he did not rest till he had found another king to fight for him. Then he marched against Rome once more, with the armies of thirty cities at his back. The Romans heard with terror of the approach of this great force, for they feared that they would not be able to beat back so many enemies; and to meet their danger, they thought it best to make a change in their government.

They had found that sometimes the two consuls could not agree, and that the state was weakened by their quarrels. So, in order to prevent this from happening now, while their freedom was to be fought for again, they determined to try another plan. They elected one man to fill the place of a king while the danger lasted, and they called him a Dictator. Every one was to obey him, as though he were a king in truth; and when he led the army out to fight against

King Tarquin and his friends once more, the people hoped that they would win the victory.

For a time, however, it seemed that they would be defeated. The soldiers fought bravely, and the Dictator made every effort to win the battle, but in spite of this the men were obliged to give way. Then the Dictator prayed to the twin gods, Castor and Pollux, and vowed to build a temple to them in Rome if they would give their help. Even as he prayed, two youths, on horses as white as snow, rode to the front of the Roman army, and began to press the enemy back, driving them at last to their camp. But when the Romans had gained their victory, and turned to look for the youths who had saved the day for them, they could find no sign of them except a hoof-print upon a rock, such as could have been made by no earthly steed.

When the army returned to Rome, however, the old men and the women, who had been left in the city, had a wonderful story to tell. While they waited in the Forum for news of the army, two strangers on white horses, covered with the foam of battle, had suddenly appeared and ridden to the pool of water by the temple of Vesta. There they had dismounted and bathed their weary horses, while they told the people of the victory of Rome. When one of the men who had gathered about them doubted the report which they brought—for it seemed too good to be true,—the youths had smiled and gently touched his beard with their hands; and that which before had been perfectly black was changed to the color of bronze. Then all had believed the good news; and the youths had mounted again and ridden away, to be seen no more.

When the Dictator heard this story, he could no longer doubt that his prayer had been answered. The two youths who had aided the army, and who had brought the news of the victory to Rome, could have been no other than the gods to whom he prayed. So a temple was built to Castor and Pollux, where they were said to have washed their horses, and some of its columns are standing on the spot to-day.

After this battle, Tarquin the Proud was unable to get any one to help him make war on Rome. Two years later he died, and after that there were no more attempts to restore the rule of the Tarquins in the City of the Seven Hills.

VII

Secession of the Plebeians.

DURING these hundreds of years since the founding of the city, Rome had been growing steadily, in spite of many wars with her enemies. It was not only that her boys and girls grew up to be men and women with children of their own, and in this way increased the number of people in the city; many persons came to Rome from other places and settled there. Sometimes they did this because the River Tiber made it a good place in which to carry on trade; and often they came because upon the well-fortified hills of the city they could be safe from robbers. Sometimes, too, the Romans would conquer the people of another town in battle, and would bring them in a body to live at Rome. So from many causes the number of the people in the city grew, until it was said that, about the time when King Tarquin was driven out, there were as many as eighty thousand men who could serve in their country's wars if there was need of them.

This was a good thing for Rome in some ways, but from one point of view it was bad. The new people and their children were not allowed to take part in the government, so the Romans came to be divided into two classes. The descendants of the old families were called patricians, and they alone could hold the offices and become priests. The descendants of the newcomers were called plebeians; and, though they could own property, carry on business, and sometimes were allowed to vote, yet they could not be elected to any office and in other ways were not allowed the full rights of Roman citizens.

After King Tarquin was driven away from the city, the condition of the plebeians became worse than it had been before. The patrician consuls and the patrician Senate used their power for the good of their own class. The nobles alone were allowed to use the public land,—some of which, you will remember, was given to Horatius as a reward. But worse than this was the cruel law of debt, which was now enforced against the plebeians more harshly than ever before.

When a poor man returned from fighting in the wars of his country, he might find that the crops on his little farm outside of Rome had been destroyed by the enemy, and his cattle driven off. Then he would be obliged to borrow money of some rich patrician to help pay his taxes and support his family until another harvest could be gathered. But, if war followed during the next summer, as often happened, he would have to leave his farm again, and so could not pay his debt when he had promised. Then he might be seized and put into prison, or even sold as a slave, by the man to whom he owed the money.

In this way, many plebeians suffered from the harsh laws, and they became very discontented. At last, one day, an old soldier appeared in the market-place appealing to the people in his great misery. His clothes were soiled and torn, and his hair and beard had grown long and shaggy over his pale, thin face.

But in spite of his pitiful appearance he was recognized as a man who had been a brave officer in the army, and on his body could be seen many scars which he had gained in the battles of Rome.

"While I have been fighting in your wars," he cried, "the enemy have destroyed the crops upon my land; they have burned my house and driven off my cattle. The money which I was compelled to borrow, I could not pay back. So my farm has been taken from me. I have been thrown into prison, and see, here are the marks of the whip upon my back!"

When the people heard his story and saw his wretched condition, a great tumult arose. The plebeians rushed upon the houses of the patricians and set free the prisoners whom they found in them. Soon, men who had suffered likewise gathered from every side, and the market-place was filled with angry shouts.

In the midst of this trouble news came that their enemies, the Volscians, were on the march toward Rome. At first the plebeians refused to enlist in the army, which was called to go out to fight them. When they were promised, however, that the laws about debts should be changed, they gave in their names and marched away to the war. Then, when the Volscians had been defeated, and the soldiers had returned, the patricians refused to change the laws as they had promised. After a great deal of trouble, the plebeians saw that they must take the matter into their own hands, but they did not become enraged and seek to gain their rights by burning and killing. You have seen that the Romans learned two things under their kings,—to fight and to obey. They had come to believe that they must submit to their laws and their rulers even if they were cruel and unjust; and, although they were now greatly abused, they did not think of taking arms against the men who governed them.

"We cannot use force against our consuls," they said, "but we will leave the patricians to fight for themselves when the next enemy comes marching against the city. We will let them receive the wounds and bear the evils from which we have been suffering."

Then they went away, and set up an armed camp on the Sacred Mount, which was not far from Rome. There they waited quietly for many days, without attacking any one and taking only enough food from the people around them to keep themselves from starving.

Meanwhile, in Rome, the consuls and the Senate were dismayed. The main support of the state was gone, and the patricians began to realize how much they had depended upon the plebeians for the good of the city. There was nothing now to stand between them and an enemy, and they trembled to think what would become of Rome if an army should march against it. When they heard that the men upon the Sacred Mount were talking of beginning a new town, as Romulus and his companions had done, they felt that they must give way, or else ruin their city and themselves. At last, they sent one of their number out to the people, offering to make terms with them. This messenger was a wise and eloquent man, and he had been chosen because he was beloved by the common people. The plebeians welcomed him to their camp, and listened to him eagerly.   He began by telling them a story.

"Once upon a time," he said, "the other parts of the human body began to grumble because they had all the work to do, while the stomach lay idle in their midst, and enjoyed the results of their labors. So they agreed that the hands should not carry food to the mouth, or the mouth receive it, or the teeth chew it. In this way, they thought to starve the stomach into submission. But soon they found that the different members, and even the entire body itself, began to grow weak and thin, and that, the more they starved the stomach, the weaker they all became. Then they began to see that the service of the stomach was by no means a small one; that it not only received nourishment, but supplied it to all the parts, and that the members of the body could not themselves live and do their work without it."

As you can easily see, the messenger meant to show the people, by this fable, that the inhabitants of a city form one great body, with each class depending upon every other for its welfare. The people listened patiently to him, and saw the truth in what he said. In the end, they returned to Rome, but only after the patricians had agreed that, from this time on, the plebeians should have a number of officers of their own, called tribunes, to protect them.

These tribunes were given very high powers. When anything was being done, even if it were by the consuls themselves, they could step forth and say, "Veto!" which means, "I forbid it!" and this command could check the action of the mightiest men in

Rome. The life and safety of the tribunes were protected by the state, and during the year that they held office, they always slept in their own houses in the city, with their doors open day and night, so that no one might seek their aid in vain.

With the tribunes to help them in their difficulties, the common people were relieved of many of their troubles. But still the struggle between the patricians and the plebeians lasted for nearly two hundred years longer, and did not cease until the plebeians had been given equal rights in the government with the patricians. Through all this long struggle there was very little bloodshed, and there was never war between the two classes. Even when the struggle was at its fiercest, the patricians and plebeians would often put aside their own quarrels, and march out, side by side, to fight the enemies of their city.

In these contests the Romans learned something better than how to fight battles successfully,—they learned to govern themselves. The patricians always held out for their rights just as long as they could, but when they were beaten, they knew how to give way and make the best of it. From these struggles the whole people learned obedience and self-control, and so became fit to rule themselves, and other lands also, when they grew strong enough to conquer them.

VIII

The Story of Coriolanus.

NOT long after the people had gained their tribunes to protect them, a noble lady, named Veturia, lived in Rome. She was a widow, and had but one son, Caius Marcius, whom she loved very dearly. From his babyhood, Caius was a strong, brave boy, and his mother had every reason to be gratified with him, except for one fault. He had a violent temper which he never learned to control; and, in the end, this brought great trouble upon both his mother and himself.

Caius was proud of his mother, and proud of his station in life as a member of the highest class in the city. From his very boyhood he tried to make himself worthy of both. At that time, almost the only training of a young Roman was for war, and the stories say that Caius labored so faithfully to learn the use of weapons, and to make his body strong, that there was soon no youth in the city who could equal him.

At last, the time came when Caius Marcius went to his first battle, and in this he proved himself to be a good fighter, although he was still almost a boy. He came back to his mother with a crown of oak leaves upon his head,—a distinction by which the Romans honored those of their soldiers who had not only fought bravely in battle, but who had also succeeded in saving the life of a Roman citizen. You may be sure that the heart of the lady Veturia was glad and proud, when she saw her son riding home to her from his first battle, with the wreath of honor upon his brow. But she had still greater cause to rejoice later, for, as time went on, and Marcius was called to fight for his city again and again, she never once saw him return without honors and rewards.

At one time, when Marcius was fighting with the Roman army, they were besieging the city of Corioli, in the country of the Volscians. As the soldiers lay camped about the city, they heard that a large force was marching to attack them from the rear. The consul, who was leading the Romans, did not wish to be caught between the walls of Corioli and a fresh army, and thus to be engaged on both sides at once. So he divided his force into two parts, and left the smaller to watch the town, while he marched against the army of the Volscians with the other.

When the people of Corioli saw that only a portion of the Roman army was left to besiege their city, they came rushing out from their gates to attack them. The Romans were driven back, and they would have been defeated if it had not been for Marcius. So fiercely did he return the attack of the enemy that they were forced to give way before him, and he encouraged his companions to pursue the flying soldiers to their gates. Even there he was not willing to stop, but, still urging his men onward, he rushed into Corioli after the defeated enemy, and kept them at bay, and the gates open, until the rest of the army could come up and take the city.

Then, as though he had done nothing to give him need of rest, he led a part of his men to help the consul in the fight against the Volscians. They arrived just as the battle was beginning, and fought bravely with the others until the victory was won. After the battle was over, Marcius was offered much rich booty as a reward, but this he would not take. He accepted only the horse of the consul, which was pressed upon him as a gift, and asked but one favor.

"I have one request to make," he said, "and this I hope you will not deny me. There is a friend of mine among the Volscian prisoners, a man of virtue, who has often entertained me at his house. He has lost his wealth and his freedom, and is now to be sold as a common slave. Let me beg that this may not be done, and that I may be allowed to save him from this last misfortune."

The consul granted this request, and Marcius returned to Rome with no other reward than this for his brave deed. But, in honor of what he had done, the people gave him a third name, which was formed from that of the city which he had taken; and, after this, he was called Caius Marcius Coriolanus. His mother, who was as proud as Coriolanus himself, must have been better pleased with this title for her son than if he had brought home a great treasure to enrich the family.

If Coriolanus could have been always with the army, doing such brave deeds, the rest of his story might have been very different. But, as he was a Roman patrician, he was not only a soldier, but one of the rulers of the city as well. The proud, fierce temper,

which Marcius had shown even in his boyhood began
to exhibit itself more and more plainly as he grew to
be an older man and took more part in the affairs of
the city.

He thought that only the patricians should have part
in the government of Rome, and he hated the tribunes,
who could check the patrician consuls by their veto.
This made the plebeians fear him, and, though the
nobles admired him for his courage, and wished to
make him consul, the people refused to elect him.
Marcius was bitterly angry over this defeat, and was
never willing to forget that he had been so slighted
after his services to the city.

Then a time came when the dislike which Coriolanus had for the plebeians made him do an unwise
thing, which proved to be his ruin. On account of
the many wars which had laid waste the fields, there
was not enough grain raised on the lands of Rome to
feed her people; and the consuls sent even as far as
Sicily for corn to keep the city from famine until the
next harvest time. But when this grain came to
Rome, it seemed to bring more trouble than comfort
to the starving citizens; for Coriolanus proposed to the
Senate that they should not allow the poor people to
receive it until they had promised to give up their
tribunes, and be governed entirely by the patricians
as before. Some of the senators were wise enough to
see that this would never do, and when the people
arose, and threatened the Senate, it gave way in spite
of Coriolanus, and allowed the corn to be sold at a low
price.

But the people were not satisfied with receiving

their grain. They now so feared and hated **Corio-lanus**, for having tried to starve them into giving up their rights, that they would no longer have him in their city. He was brought to trial by the tribunes, and the people sentenced him to banishment for life.

Coriolanus went away with his heart full of bitterness. He could not see that he had been wrong, and he felt only hatred now for the Roman people, who, as it seemed to him, had abused and mistreated him. He went, therefore, to the country of the Volscians, against whom he had fought so many battles for the Romans. At the fall of night, he came to the house of one of their chiefs. There he entered and seated himself as a suppliant at the hearth, with his mantle covering his face. He had such an air of pride and sorrow that the members of the family did not dare to question him, but sent for Tullus, the master of the house. When Tullus went to him, asking him who he was and for what purpose he had come, Coriolanus arose and threw the covering from his head.

"Do you not remember me?" he said, looking him proudly in the face. "I am that Caius Marcius who has brought so much trouble upon the Volscians. If I were to deny this my name of Coriolanus would still declare me your enemy. That name is the one thing which I received in reward for my perils and hardships in battles, and it is the one thing that the Romans have left me, as they send me forth an exile. Now I come, an humble suppliant at your hearth, not for protection, but for revenge. Let me lead your people against the Romans, and you will have the advantage of a general who knows all the secrets of your enemies.

If I may not do this, let me perish as your foe, for I no longer wish to live."

Tullus was rejoiced to give him what he asked, and soon Coriolanus marched against Rome with a Volscian army at his back. When he came near the city, the Romans were terror-stricken, for they felt too weak to contend with their old enemies, when led by their own general. The senators and the people, therefore, agreed to send messengers to Coriolanus, offering to restore him to his place at Rome, and begging him not to bring the terror and distress of war upon his city. These messengers were chosen from among his friends and relatives in order that they might have more influence with him. But he treated them harshly, as if he had altogether forgotten his former love for them, and would hear no word of peace. Then the Romans sent all the priests, clothed in their sacred robes, to plead with him; but they also were turned away.

At this the city was given over to despair, for the people felt that there was no cruelty of the harshest enemy that could be compared with the fierce wrath of the exiled Coriolanus. The old men knelt weeping at the altars of the gods, and the women ran wailing through the streets of the city. But when all other help had failed them, Veturia, the proud mother of Coriolanus, roused herself from her sorrow. She gathered around her the noblest of the Roman women, placing her son's wife and his children by her side, and set out with them for the camp of the Volscians.

Coriolanus saw the women coming as suppliants through his camp, but he watched them unmoved, until he recognized his mother at their head. Then his proud soul was shaken, and he ran to her with his arms outstretched, as though he were the young Caius once more. But his mother drew back and addressed him sternly.

"Do I behold you, my son," she said, "in arms against the walls of Rome? Tell me, before I receive your embrace, whether I am in your camp as a captive or as your mother. Does length of life give me only this, to behold my son an exile and an enemy? If I had not been a mother, Rome would not have been besieged! If I had not had a son, I might die free, in a free country! But be sure of this, my son, that you shall not be able to reach your country to harm it, unless you first cross the body of your mother."

As she spoke these words, she threw herself upon the ground at the feet of Coriolanus. a suppliant before her own son. But Marcius, weeping, raised her from the earth.

"O Mother! what is this that you have done to me! You have saved Rome, but destroyed your son. I go, conquered by you alone."

Then he led his army away; and it is said that he met his death at the hands of the disappointed Volscians. Veturia, meanwhile, returned in loneliness to Rome, mourning for her beloved son; though like the Consul Brutus she held her child less dear than the freedom of her country.

IX

The Family of the Fabii.*

THE family of the Fabii, and, indeed, all the families of Rome, were very different from our own American families, or any others that you may know about. You think of your family as being made up of your father and mother, brothers and sisters, and, it may be, a grandfather or a grandmother who lives with you. You have other relatives, of course, —uncles, aunts, and cousins; but perhaps these live far away in some other part of the country, and you may know very little about them. Even if you have a family of relatives living in the same town with you, you do not think of them as belonging to your own family, as your brothers and sisters do.

This was all quite different in the city of Rome. There the families were held closer together than with us, and cousins that were so distantly related that we should scarcely think them cousins at all, were all counted in the great family to which their fathers and grandfathers and great-grandfathers had belonged for centuries before them. This made the families very large,—as large, perhaps, as your own would be if you

---

* Many Latin words ended in the letters "us" in the singular number. To make the plural of such words, the "us" was changed to "i." In this way, the name "Fabius," in the singular number becomes "Fabii" when we wish to speak of more than one person.

could go back through your grandfathers to the first one who came to America, and then should gather together all the persons in the country to-day who are related to him, however distantly.

If you will only think for a moment of how many this might be, you will not be surprised to find that the family of the Fabii, counting men, women, and children, is supposed to have contained many hundreds of persons. Of course, all these people did not live in the same house, as we think of families doing to-day, for that would have been impossible. But they all bore the name of Fabius, and they all obeyed the head of their family more readily than sons nowadays obey their own fathers.

The Fabii belonged to the patrician class, and were richer and more powerful than any other family in Rome; so, year after year, some one of them was sure to be elected consul. At last, the common people grew weary of this, especially as the Fabii always opposed the tribunes in everything that they wished to do for the good of the people. The plebeians grew to dislike the family so much that they were willing to do anything to distress and annoy them.

While the people were in this humor, Kæso Fabius, who was then one of the consuls, led the Roman army against the enemy. He left the city with his horsemen and foot soldiers, and drew up his men before the enemy's camp. He was a good general, and everything was well arranged for the battle, when he gave the signal for the attack; but, at his command, the cavalry alone, who were all patricians, obeyed and went against the foe. The plebeians, who were the foot soldiers, hated their consul so much that they stood still and refused to go forward and take their part in the battle. They did this because they wished to see their consul go back to Rome disgraced by defeat, and in fact he did return without glory, bearing only the increased ill-will of his soldiers. Then, though the Fabii were proud and haughty men, they saw that they had gone too far in their harshness toward the common people.

When some of Rome's neighbors heard of the trouble among the people, they agreed that this would be a good time to lead their forces against the city while it was thus weakened by dissensions. So, during the next year, another force, from several places, came marching together against Rome. The Senate was greatly distressed at this, for one of the consuls was again a Fabius, and they had no way of making sure that the soldiers would not behave as they had done the year before. Indeed, they left home with a sullen look, as though they were determined to show their anger again, even at the risk of bringing ruin upon the city. For this reason, the consuls were afraid to trust their men in battle; so when they came near the enemy, they pitched their camp, and fortified it, and kept their soldiers quietly within it.

Day by day, and week by week, the army lay within its camp. The enemies of the Romans now began to think that there was trouble again between the patricians and the people, and that the soldiers had once more refused to fight. They were delighted at this, and felt as though the victory was already won.

Often they would come close to the Roman camp and scoff at the soldiers who lay within.

"You pretend to disagree, so that you may not show how afraid of us you are," they would call, mockingly. "Your consuls fear to lead you to battle, for they distrust your courage even more than your obedience."

The Romans could not endure these insults long. Soon, the men who had come out determined not to fight, were begging their consuls to lead them against the enemy. But Fabius did not think that they had been sufficiently disciplined, and he only replied:

"The time has not yet come."

So the soldiers were still forced to remain closely in their camp, and hear the taunting cries of the enemy, who called, "Cowards, cowards," and, at last, threatened to attack the camp itself. Then, when the Romans were all afire with anger and impatience, and Fabius saw that they could no longer be kept from attacking the enemy who insulted them, he drew the army up and spoke to them.

"Soldiers, I know that you are able to conquer these men who mock you; but what makes me hesitate to give battle is the doubt whether you will do it, or will stand still in the face of the enemy, as you did last year. I have, therefore, determined not to give the signal for battle until you will swear by the gods that you will return victorious. Our soldiers have once deceived the Roman consuls; the gods they will never deceive."

Then one of the foremost soldiers raised his hand and cried:

"Fabius, I will return victorious from the field or die upon it. If I deceive you, may the anger of Jupiter, Mars, and all the gods be upon me."

Following his example, the whole army took the same oaths. They were then led forth to battle, and, after a hard fight, during which the soldiers were faithful to the last, they defeated the enemy.

After this, the Fabian family tried rather to favor the poorer people than to be harsh and stern in their treatment of them. Kæso Fabius ordered all the soldiers who were wounded in this battle to be cared for in the houses of the rich; and in the homes of the Fabii, these men were treated more kindly than anywhere else. Little by little, the people forgot their hatred and began to look upon the great family as their friends. For their part, the Fabii soon proved that, however proud they might be, they were willing to sacrifice everything for the safety of their city.

There came a time when all the enemies of Rome seemed to be taking up arms against her at once, and the people were overburdened with the preparations for meeting so many foes, in so many different directions. As the Senate was anxiously discussing the means of providing against the danger, Kæso Fabius arose, and spoke for all the Fabian family.

"Fathers, do you attend to the other wars. Appoint the Fabii as the enemies of the Veientians. We pledge ourselves that the honor of the Roman name shall be safe in that quarter. And, as we ask this war for our family, it is our plan to conduct it at our own expense; for the city, which is so burdened with other dangers, should be spared the expense of soldiers and of supplies in this direction.''

The Senate accepted this offer with joy and thankfulness, and the next day the Fabii left the town. There were three hundred and six men, all patricians and all Fabii, in this little army. The people, quite forgetting their former dislike of the family, followed them through the streets of the city; and, at the altar of each god, they begged that the brave men might go forth to victory, and return safely to their homes once more.

These prayers, however, were all in vain. No one of that little company ever came back to Rome. They went out and built a fort facing the lands of their enemies, and kept them in check for many months. But at last they were surprised and overcome by them, and the whole army of the Fabii was put to death. Only one boy who had been too young to go with his relatives. remained of that great family of brave men. But this boy became, in time, the head of another Fabian family, which was to win as much honor at Rome as the one that had been destroyed.

X

The Victory of Cincinnatus.

ON the slopes of the mountains east of Rome, **there** lived a sturdy people called the Æquians. The Romans had to contend with this nation for many years after the expulsion of their kings. As soon as one war with them was ended, another was sure to begin; and it was during one of these many struggles that a Roman called Cincinnatus made his name famous among the heroes of the early city.

It happened once that a band of these Æquians marched into the Roman lands, and began to burn and plunder on every side. A treaty of peace had been made between the Romans and the Æquians only the year before; so the Senate sent some citizens to the intruders, to complain of their conduct. When these messengers reached the camp of the Æquians, they found the chiefs of the band sitting in the shade of a great oak tree.

"Why do you come into our lands," they asked, "making war in time of peace, and breaking the treaty which you have made with us? The Roman Senate demands that you make a return for what you have destroyed, and leave the country in peace."

The leader of the Æquians would hear no more than this

"The Roman Senate!" he exclaimed **in scorn.**

"Deliver to this oak tree whatever instructions you have brought from the Roman Senate, and in the meantime, I will attend to other matters!" And he turned to leave them.

Then the Roman messengers also prepared to depart, for they saw that nothing could be done in the way of a peaceful settlement. But as they left one of them cried:

"Let both this sacred oak and all the gods be wit-

ROMAN PLOUGH.

nesses that the treaty is broken by you. So may they help our arms presently, when we shall seek to avenge ourselves!"

They went away, and soon a Roman consul led an army against the Æquians. This consul was not a brave and ready man, as most of the Romans were, and the Æquians soon discovered that he was afraid to come to battle with them. Then they laid siege to his camp and by throwing up earthworks around it, they had his army as safe as if in a trap. Five of the Romans, however, succeeded in passing through the lines of the enemy, and hurried to the city with the news that the army was surrounded.

When the Romans heard this the Senate was hurriedly called together, and decided that a Dictator must be appointed. Lucius Quintius, who was called "Cincinnatus," on account of his crisp, curly hair, was the one whom they chose to meet their present difficulty.

Cincinnatus, though he was a good soldier and a patrician, was a poor man, and tilled his own little farm of four acres on the other side of the River Tiber. When the messengers of the Senate came, early in the morning, to announce to him that he had been appointed Dictator, they found him ploughing in the fields without his "toga," or outer gown. Before telling him their business, they bade him leave his work, and put on his toga, that he might listen with due respect to the commands of the Senate.

At this, Cincinnatus was astonished, and asked frequently whether anything was the matter, while his wife brought his toga from the cottage. Then washing himself free from the dust and sweat of his work, he wrapped himself in his gown, as though he were in the Senate house, and listened to the messengers.

They saluted him as Dictator, and, explaining the trouble in the city, they bade him come to Rome and take the command. Cincinnatus obeyed, and went with them to the town, where he was met at the gates by his sons; then, with twenty-four lictors marching on before him, he was escorted to his house in the city.

When the next day dawned, Cincinnatus went into the assembly of the people and declared that business must be stopped,—that everyone must now attend only to the affairs of the State. Then he commanded that all who were of the age to act as soldiers should come together in the Field of Mars before sunset, each bringing twelve large wooden stakes besides his arms and food for five days. Those who were too old to act as soldiers he ordered to prepare the food for the other men, while these were busy cutting the stakes.

When the appointed time came, the men set out, with Cincinnatus marching before them, and bidding them hasten.

"The consul and his army have now been besieged three days," he said. "It is uncertain what each day and night may bring with it. You must hasten, that we may reach the camp this very night, for often the gain of a moment will change defeat into victory."

And the men, to please their leader and encourage themselves, called to one another:

"Follow, soldiers! Hasten on!"

At midnight they reached the camp, where the Æquians were laying siege to the Romans. Cincinnatus first rode all around the place in order to discover, as well as he could in the darkness, how it was arranged. Then he drew his men silently in a long column around the camp, directing that at a signal, they should raise a shout, and begin digging a trench and driving their stakes before it for defense.

When all was ready, the signal was given; and their cries rose though the silent night, terrifying the Æquians, and carrying joy to tne hearts of the imprisoned consul and his army. These sprang to their feet, exclaiming:

"That is the shout of our countrymen! Help is at hand! Let us also attack the enemy!"

Then they seized their arms, and rushed upon the Æquians just as they were turning to attack the soldiers of Cincinnatus. It was scarcely daylight before the Romans had conquered; for the Æquians were attacked from both sides at once, and were fighting unknown numbers in the darkness of the night.

After the battle was over, the enemies of the Romans were not destroyed, for Cincinnatus said:

"I want not the blood of the Æquians. Let them depart in peace. But, before they go, we must have a confession that their nation is defeated and subdued. They must all pass under the yoke."

Then he ordered two spears to be driven into the earth, and a third one fastened across their tops. Under this the Æquians were obliged to pass, without their arms, and with but one garment on their backs, to show to all the world that they were now as peaceful and subdued as the patient oxen that ploughed the Roman fields with the yoke upon their necks.

Cincinnatus then prepared to return to Rome at once. He gave all the booty of the Æquian camp to his own soldiers, and punished the consul for his cowardice by giving him and his soldiers nothing. When they reached the city, they found it full of joy at the rescue of its army. The Senate voted that Cincinnatus should enter Rome in triumph. So he marched into the city by the "Gate of Triumph," with the chiefs of the Æquians led before him, and the standards of the army carried around his car. The soldiers followed after, loaded down with their booty. Tables covered with provisions are said to have been laid out before the houses of all, and the soldiers were fed in abundance, as they followed the car of their general with shouts and rejoicing.

Cincinnatus, however, was not over-exalted by his great victory and by the honor that was shown him afterwards. On the sixteenth day after he had received the command, he laid down his power, and returned to his little farm and his ploughing. For this simple act he has been as much admired as for his great success as a general.

At the close of the Revolutionary War, Washington and his companions did the same thing that Cincinnatus was praised for doing so many centuries before them. They gave up their places as generals and officers in the army, and went peacefully back to their farms and shops again. They thought of Cincinnatus at the time, and joined together to form a society which they called "the Cincinnati," after this old Roman. This society, in its turn, gave its name to a city which bears it yet, the city of Cincinnati, in the state of Ohio. From this you can see how long a man's name may last in the world, if he is only strong and noble enough to do something which people will be glad to remember always.

XI

The Laws of the Twelve Tables.

AS you read these tales of the early heroes you may think, perhaps, that the teaching of King Numa was wasted; that the Romans after him did nothing but fight, and studied nothing but the art of winning battles. Most of the oldest stories that have come down to us tell only of the defeat or victory of a Roman army,—for that seemed the one important thing to the men who wrote the records. This, however, did not make up all the life of the Roman people. They were something else besides soldiers: they were citizens of Rome, and members of family groups; and much might have been told us about their life in the city of which we shall always be ignorant.

The wisest men among the Romans at this time knew very little about the world, even as it was then; and, if they had considered it deeply, they could never have imagined what people who might be living more than two thousand years after they were dead would like best to know about them. They only thought, as they wrote their records, that by the favor of the gods their city should last forever, and that, in later years, their own people might have forgotten when some town was taken, or how some army had been destroyed. So they wrote down these facts, and made them as lasting as they could; and they did not know that, after twenty centuries, people would rather learn more of how they bought and sold in their market places, and prayed in their temples, and behaved to one another in their homes, than so much about their little armies, and the towns that they destroyed.

The account of the Twelve Tables of the Law, however, does not concern itself with battles. In it you will hear of no consul leading his soldiers out of the city to meet the enemy, and of no Dictator returning in triumph, having gained a victory for his country. It is not a tale of war, but of the beginning of written law among the Romans, and it is a much nobler story than that of any of their sieges.

When we Americans speak of the "law," we think of the statutes which are printed in many books, and which are used by our judges and lawyers in trying cases in our courts. The Romans, at first, did not know anything of this kind of law. Such rules as they had were all unwritten, and were only known to the patricians who had handed them down by word of mouth from father to son, for many hundreds of years. The common people did not know them, and they had no way of finding out what was right for them to do, except by asking some one who had been taught the law from his early youth.

This might not have been so hard for the common people if all the patricians had learned the same law. and used their knowledge justly. But there were many different rules about the same thing, and the men who wished to be unfair could choose the law that would be most to their advantage, and of the least help to the people who appealed to them. By this crooked dealing, the people were often misled and treated very unjustly by the patricians; but as they did not know the law, and had no way of learning it, they could do nothing to help themselves.

It was one of the tribunes of the people who at last tried to aid them by giving them the knowledge that was lacking to them. He proposed that all the laws of Rome should be gathered together and published, so that the people could understand what they must and must not do, and so avoid making mistakes because of ignorance. The patricians of Rome were opposed to this, for they did not wish to share their knowledge of the law with the plebeians. They felt that this would be yielding even more of their rights over the people than had been surrendered when they were brought back from the Sacred Mount and given their tribunes to protect them.

For this reason, the Senate refused to consent to the publishing of the law. But the people had now learned to be as firm in what they demanded as the Senate. Year after year, they elected only those men for tribunes who promised to help them in this struggle; and year after year, the tribunes continued to demand patiently and firmly the publication of the laws. It was ten years, however, before the Senate finally gave up the struggle and allowed the people to have their own way. Then they all agreed upon a curious thing. They changed their whole government for the time during which the laws were to be written; and instead of electing consuls and tribunes, as usual, they chose ten men who were both to govern the city and prepare the laws for the people.

After working together for some time over their task, these men called the people together and said to them:

"We have written the laws as justly toward the highest and the lowest as it can be done by the consideration of ten men. The understanding and advice of a greater number might prove more successful. We bid you, therefore, go and read the laws that are placed before you. Consider them in your own minds in each particular, and talk together concerning them, in order that you may discover everything in which they are at fault. For we wish you to seem not to have accepted the laws proposed for you, but to have proposed them for yourselves."

The people hastened to do as they were bidden. When the laws had been considered by all and the faults seemed to have been corrected, they were approved by the assembly of the people, and published so that all men might see them. But perhaps you will wonder how they could be published in an age without printing presses and books, such as we have now. The Romans used a simple plan for this, but one that answered very well. They carved their laws upon twelve tablets of bronze, and then hung them in their market-place, or Forum, as they called it, on the sides of the stand from which the Romans made their speeches to the assembly of the people.

Here, in this public place, every man who could read was free to come and study them. As the Forum was the busiest place in Rome, where each citizen came at some time during almost every day of his life in the city, you will see that, after this, they lived with their laws constantly before their eyes. The boys, too, were obliged to learn the Twelve Tables by heart, as part of their education, and we may easily believe that it was not hard for a bright boy, who would be glad for an excuse to linger in the bustling Forum, to learn the whole contents of the tables long before he could take part in his first battle. Certainly, there was no excuse now for the Romans of any class not to know what was lawful and unlawful; and in this way a nobler thing had been done than if they had conquered many cities, and sold their inhabitants into slavery.

These bronze tablets of the law have not come down to us through the centuries, as some of the Roman buildings have done. They were broken and destroyed long ago; but most of their contents have been preserved for us in the writings of the later Romans. Some of these laws seem remarkable to us now, who are living with such different manners and customs; and this, perhaps, is most true of the laws that concern the family.

The father of the Roman family was like a ruler in a little kingdom all his own, in which no one, not even the consul, could interfere. He could do exactly as he pleased with his wife and his children and his servants. His children never became independent of their father, as you will be of yours when you become of age. The Roman father kept his power over his sons and daughters until the day of his death, and the laws even allowed him to sell his children as slaves, or to hire them out to work for his profit, whether they wished to do so or not.

But besides the laws which seem to us so strange, there were many which appear more reasonable.

Among these was one which declared that if a tree overhung the ground of a neighbor, he might take the fruit that dropped on his side of the line. If any one cut down the trees which belonged to another, he must pay twenty-five pounds of copper for each tree; and a man who turned cattle into a neighbor's growing crop, or reaped his grain by night, was to be severely punished.

As time went on, some of the laws of the twelve tables were changed and a great many others were added to them. Then it became impossible for any one to learn all of them by heart, and at last the boys ceased to learn even the laws of the twelve tables. But the main principles of the Roman laws remained the same under every change; they were only made clearer, and juster, and better fitted to the changes in the world to which they were to be applied. So they survived when almost everything else of the Roman rule had passed away, and they are still the foundation of the law in Italy, France, Spain, and even in our own state of Louisiana.

XII

How Camillus Captured Veii.

ABOUT twenty miles north of Rome was a large and powerful city called Veii, with which the Romans were often at war. It was in a struggle with this town that the Fabii had been destroyed; and after that, war had followed war, until the fourteenth conflict was under way. During this the Romans had laid siege to the town for eight long years, and it seemed as though they would never be able to conquer it. The Senate and the people had all become discouraged, when a strange thing happened to make them still more anxious and disturbed.

About as far south of Rome as Veii was north of it, lay the Alban Lake, which was completely surrounded by hills, and had no inlet or outlet for its waters. News now came to Rome that the water of this lake had suddenly begun to rise higher and higher, without heavy rains, or any other cause that could be discovered. The Romans, therefore, imagined that this was a miracle which was performed by the gods; and to find out the meaning of it, they sent messengers to the Oracle of the god Apollo, at Delphi. But before these messengers had returned, they received an explanation of the matter from the Veientians themselves.

As often happens in long sieges, the soldiers of the two armies had formed the habit of calling back and forth at one another. One day, as they were doing this, an old man stood upon the walls of Veii and declared, like one uttering a prophecy, that "until the waters should be discharged from the Alban Lake, the Romans should never become the masters of Veii."

One of the Roman soldiers caught at this saying eagerly, thinking that perhaps it showed a way for them to become at last victorious. He persuaded the old man to come out from the walls, and talk with him in the open ground before the Roman camp; then, when they were alone, he seized him boldly about the waist, and carried him by main force into the camp. From there he was taken to the Senate at Rome, and commanded to repeat the prophecy which he had spoken upon the walls of his city. He replied:

"The gods were angry with the Veientian people that day, when they bade me show the way to ruin my country from the walls of Veii. But, since it seemed to them well for me to speak it, it is better said than unsaid. It is written in the books of the fates that whenever the Alban water shall rise to a great height, and the Romans shall discharge it in the proper manner, victory will be granted to them. Until that is done, the gods will not desert the walls of Veii."

When the Romans found that the answer of the Oracle of Apollo agreed with the statement of the old man, they set eagerly to work to do what was required of them. While some remained with the army to watch about the walls of Veii, others worked at the Alban Lake. To make a passage for the imprisoned waters through the rock of the hills, they cut a great tunnel, the remains of which can still be traced.

Ditches were then dug through the country and the water of the lake was let out upon the fields.

After all this was done, a Roman named Camilius was appointed Dictator, to complete the capture of the city When he reached the place he withdrew the Romans into their camp, and kept them closely there, in order that there might be no chance for speech with the enemy. Then he began a tunnel which was to lead from the camp, under the walls of the city, and into the very heart of the town. Day and night his soldiers worked at this, each in his turn, so that no one should become exhausted by the hard labor. At last the task was all completed, except breaking through the last thin crust of earth which would admit them into the city.

The Veientians still laughed and shouted from their walls at the silent Romans, all unconscious that the Alban Lake had disappeared into the earth, and that their enemies were ready to pour into the city from their tunnel. But Camillus was certain of his victory, and having given orders for the soldiers to take their arms, he went forth to beg the help and favor of the gods.

"Under thy guidance, O Apollo," he prayed, "I proceed to destroy the city of Veii, and I vow to thee a tenth part of the spoil."

Then some of his army was sent against the walls. As the Veientians rushed to their defense, others of the Romans came out of the tunnel in the city and attacked them from behind. The Veientians were taken by surprise, and the Romans within soon succeeded in opening the gates of the town for their companions. By this means they won a complete victory, and, after the custom of ancient warfare, made slaves of the people who had withstood them so bravely, and stripped their town of all its treasures.

Then the Romans prepared to remove the gods also

JUNO.

from the captured city. A band of young men was chosen, and, with their bodies freshly washed in pure water and clad in white garments, they took their way in a solemn procession to the temple of the great Juno. She was the especial god of the Veientians, and they entered her house with fear and awe. When they stood before the image of the goddess, one of the company asked:

"O Juno, art thou willing to go to Rome?"

Then the youths believed that they saw the goddess ɔow her beautiful head in assent, and they all shouted with joy. They took up the statue and carried it to Rome; and they persuaded themselves that it seemed light and easy to move, as though the goddess went with them willingly and of her own accord.

For several years after this, the city of Veii was left standing with empty houses and temples, uncared for either by the gods or men. Some of the old neighbors of the Veientians, however, tried to make a stand against the Romans, even though Veii itself had fallen. So Camillus was sent against one of their cities, to lay siege to it, as he had done to Veii. This place was also a strong town, and the people seemed likely to defend themselves as long and as bravely as the Veientians had done. But, one day, the war suddenly ceased, and peace was made as a result of the just dealing of Camillus with the people of the besieged city.

Several of the noblest families of the town had placed their boys in the charge of a schoolmaster, who was expected not only to teach them, but to care for them during their playtime also. Before the war began, this man had been in the habit of taking his boys beyond the walls for play and exercise, and even when the city had been besieged he continued in this custom.

One day, when they had passed through the gates as usual for their romp in the open field, and while the boys were all absorbed in their rough play, their teacher led them little by little up to the Roman lines, and to the tent of Camillus. Then, as he came before the Roman general, he said:

"Camillus, these are the children of the men who are highest in rank in the city. With them I deliver to you the city itself, for their rulers will be willing to sacrifice everything to regain their children; and I know that you will reward me for my deed."

But Camillus would not take advantage of his treachery.

"Wicked as thou art," he cried, "thou hast not come with thy offering to a commander or a people like thyself. We do not carry arms against defenseless children, but against armed men." He then ordered the man's arms to be tied behind his back; and put rods in the boys' hands, bidding them flog their treacherous master back to the city, where he would certainly be punished as he well deserved to be.

When the people of the city received their children again from Camillus, their feeling toward the Romans changed. Before this time, they had preferred the fate of the Veientians to making peace with the Romans, but now the virtue of Camillus filled them with admiration. They sent messengers to the Roman Senate, therefore, and surrendered themselves without further struggle, saying:

"Fathers, we are overcome by your good faith, and we give the victory to you of our own free will. We believe that we shall live more happily under your rule than we do now under our own laws; so send men to receive our arms, and our city."

By two such victories as these, and many smaller ones, Camillus became one of the greatest of the

Romans. The people were grateful to him for his services to the city, and they were certain that no one could lead the Roman armies so well as he. But Camillus, like Coriolanus, was a proud man, and wished to rule the city as he did his army. Among other things, he was determined that the tenth part of the spoil of Veii should be given to Apollo, as he had promised before the battle, and this the people did not wish to do. He forced it from them at last; and then they asked him, in return, what right he had to the great bronze doors which he had brought from the conquered city, and placed before his own house.

So Camillus and the people fell to quarreling, and, after a time, the general was forced to leave Rome. In rage and sorrow, he went to find a home in another place; but he would have preferred to have lost his life in his city s battles, for to be obliged to lead the life of a exile was worse than death to a Roman.

XIII

The Coming of the Gauls.

IN all the wars which the Romans had fought up to this time, they had been contending with people who were near neighbors to them, and who were like themselves in their ways of life and methods of fighting. But six years after the capture of Veii, they were called upon to meet a new race in battle, whose like they had never seen before, and at whose hands they met a terrible defeat.

North of the peninsula of Italy, you will remember, and shutting it off from the rest of Europe, lies the great snowy chain of the Alps. These mountains are higher and more difficult to cross than any of the mountains of our own country; but there are now many well-made wagon roads through them and even some railroads. In the early days of Rome, however, there were merely paths and the great snow-covered ridges made a barrier which men rarely thought of crossing. The Romans knew nothing of the people who lived on the other side of the Alps, and perhaps would never have thought, for many centuries longer, of climbing through their rough passes to find out what lay beyond them.

But the peoples who lived north of these mountains were very different from the Italians, and were not held in one place by the love of their lands and homes.

They had villages and towns of their own; but these were poor and ill-made, compared to the Italian cities, and the people were always ready to leave them to follow their chiefs into other countries to gain new possessions. The Alps, too, are easier to climb from the north than from the south, for the slope on the northern side is much more gradual. So some of these tribes found their way over into Italy while the Romans were still absorbed by the affairs of their own city and its little neighborhood wars.

GALLIC SOLDIER.

These nations from the north had many names among themselves, but the Italians usually called them all by the name of Gauls. They were very different in appearance from any people that the Italians had ever seen. The Romans and the other Italians were small compared with the Gauls, and had black hair and eyes, and dark skins browned by the suns of the long Italian summers. The Gauls were from a more temperate climate; where the milder sunlight and the cooler summers had left their hair and skins fair and their eyes blue. This was a continual wonder to the darker Italians; and, when we consider in addition the superior size of the Gauls, it is not surprising to find that the Romans spoke with awe of these blue-eyed giants, for many years after they had disappeared from the neighborhood of Rome.

The dress of the Gauls was also strange to the Romans, for they wore garments checked and striped in many colors. These remind us of the bright tartans in which the Highlanders of Scotland clothed themselves for centuries, and of which they make some use even nowadays. Indeed, the Highlanders are, perhaps, the most closely related to these ancient Gauls of any people now in the world, and only a few hundred years ago, they were using war-horns and swords in their battles very much like the ones that the Romans tell us the Gauls brought with them into Italy.

The Gauls differed as much from the Romans in their manner of fighting as they did in their appearance. The Romans, during their long experience in warfare, had learned to draw up their soldiers in a regular form, with the cavalry and the infantry in fixed positions, and they always went into battle in an orderly manner. The Gauls never dreamed of anything like a plan in their arrangement. Each man, with his broad, unpointed sword, and long shield, took his place in the great mass of his fellow soldiers; and, when the signal for battle came, they all rushed furiously at the enemy. Those who were behind pushed on those in front, if they showed signs of giving way; and their savage yells and the din of their horns terrified the enemy as much as the blows from their heavy swords.

Some tribes of the Gauls had been settled in the northern part of Italy for a long time before the Romans heard anything about them. This is a good example of how much larger Italy was then to the people who lived in it. Now the citizens of Rome know the events in the valley of the Po almost as quickly as those of their own town, but the ancient Romans lived for years without discovering that a new race had already gained a foothold in their country. It was only when a band of the Gauls,—leaving their families behind them, with their relatives who had settled along the Po,—pushed down farther to the south, and crossed the Apennines, that they came to the knowledge of the Romans.

These Gauls were terrible destroyers; and, as they went, they left a broad path behind them, in which there were only ruined towns, and fields bare of any sign of life. City after city fell into their hands, and terror spread before them through the country. When they came to the Tuscan town of Clusium, where Lars Porsena had ruled a century before, messengers were sent to Rome to beg for help against this new enemy.

At first, Rome only replied to this request by sending three ambassadors to treat with the Gauls. When these Romans and the men of Clusium met the chiefs of the Gauls, they demanded why they had come in this manner into the country of another people.

"We want land for those of us who have none," replied the Gauls, "and the men of Clusium have more than they can use. Give us what we ask, and we will not make war upon you."

"But what right have you to ask for land from the

men of Clusium, and threaten war if they refuse it?" the Romans cried, thinking of their own lands, which might be asked for next.

"We carry our right in our swords," the Gauls replied. "All things belong to the brave. Do you stand by, O Romans, and see us decide this matter with our arms, and then carry home the story of how much the Gauls excel all other peoples in bravery."

The people of Clusium could not endure this haughty speech. They refused the demand of the Gauls, and a battle began. The Roman ambassadors, too, were angry, and this caused them to forget the law of nations, which has never allowed ambassadors to take part in actual fighting. They entered the battle, side by side with the soldiers of Clusium, and one of the three killed a chieftain of the Gauls in the sight of both the armies.

Then the Gauls were much enraged. With a sudden impulse, they ceased their attack on Clusium, and sent messengers to Rome demanding that the offenders should be given up to them for punishment. When this was refused, they marched straight upon the city.

The Romans heard of their coming, and prepared to meet them, but not so carefully as they would have done if the Gauls had been the people of some neighboring city. They did not seem to think it worth while to appoint a Dictator, as they had so often done when other dangers threatened them. They did not realize that they would have to meet an enemy more difficult to face than any they had ever fought before. Perhaps they even despised the Gauls for their savage ways, and their clumsy weapons, of which they must

have heard; and thought that it would not be so difficult to defeat men who fought with their heads
unprotected by helmets. But, if the Romans under-
rated the Gauls before they met them, they learned
from them one great lesson,—that it is never safe to
scorn an enemy, until you have tried his strength.

When the Gauls had come as near as the eleventh
milestone from the city, the Romans went out to
meet them with a large army. The battle took place
on the banks of a little stream which flows into the
river Tiber. There the Romans drew up their men
in a long line, as they were in the habit of doing when
they met their Italian enemies, without considering
whether this was the best way to withstand the mad
dash of their new foes.

With their horns blowing and their shouts rising in
a fearful roar, the Gauls came charging in a great mass
at the Roman army, and went through the line of
brave soldiers with a rush that could not be resisted.
The Romans were divided into two parts, as if a
wedge had been driven through them; and, terrified at
the savage attack and their sudden defeat, they fled
blindly, as they had so often caused their own enemies
to flee. The greater part of the Roman army was cut off
from Rome by the force of the Gauls, and the men were
obliged to throw themselves into the Tiber, and swim
to the other shore, where they took refuge behind the
walls of the deserted city of Veii. The smaller part
retreated in a panic to Rome; and, rushing through
the streets, made their way into the citadel without
stopping to close the gates behind them.

The Gauls did not pursue them. They were amazed

at their sudden success, and they hesitated to go on, for fear that there might be some trap prepared for them. They turned back, to gather up the arms of the Roman dead; and then they spent their time in dividing the spoil and feasting. As a result of this, it was not until the third day after the battle—in mid-summer, 390 B.C.—that the army of the Gauls appeared before the gates of Rome.

XIV

The Gauls in Rome.

MEANWHILE, all was terror and dismay in Rome. Only a handful of men had returned from the army that had marched out on the day of the battle. But the Romans had not only to sorrow for the dead; they had also to fear for the living, as the men who remained in Rome were too few to defend the wide extent of the city walls against the attack of these fierce barbarians.

So, without making any attempt to guard the wall, the Romans determined to take their stand on the Capitol. This was a rocky hill, upon which the citadel was built, and it was of course well fitted for defense. Its sides were so steep, except where the road ascended, that it seemed as though no enemy could climb them. Upon it was a well, to furnish a sure supply of water; and there, too, were the temples of the gods, to protect and encourage the citizens in the defense of their last stronghold.

While the Gauls gathered their spoil and feasted, the Romans hastened to bring provisions to this place and prepare it to withstand a siege. Not all of the people, however, could find refuge here. No one was wanted on the Capitol who could not do his share in its defense; the women and the children, and the people untrained to arms, would only have taken the food from the mouths of those who labored to save the most sacred part of the town.

So, while the Capitol was being made ready, great numbers of the people went out of Rome, and sought refuge in the hills on the other side of the Tiber, and in the neighboring cities. With them went the Vestal Virgins, carrying the sacred fire from the altar, and the vessels used in the worship of the gods. The Romans have preserved the story of how a poor plebeian, who was flying with his goods and family, met the Vestals as they were toiling along the road on foot; and how, seeing their weariness, he bade his wife and children get down from his cart, that he might take up the holy maidens and carry them to a place of safety.

There were some of the Romans, however, who could not fight, and yet who would not leave the city. These were the old patricians, who were too feeble to bear arms and be useful in the citadel, but who could not bear the thought of leaving their homes and wandering in exile, while the city they loved was laid in ashes by the barbarous Gauls. They determined, therefore, to make a sacrifice of themselves to the gods for the good of their country. They were men who in their earlier years had been consuls, or had filled other high offices in the city. Now they put on their robes of state, and seated themselves in their ivory chairs in the Forum, to wait calmly for the coming of the enemy.

When, at last, the Gauls entered the city, they passed wonderingly from street to street through the empty town, seeking the enemy who awaited them only in the citadel above. When they came to the Forum, they were struck with amazement at the sight of so many stately old men, sitting there in perfect order and silence. On their part, the nobles neither rose at their coming, nor so much as turned their eyes towards them, but gazed upon one another quietly, and showed no sign of fear.

For a while, the Gauls stood wondering at the strange sight, and did not approach or touch the Romans, for they seemed more like an assembly of the gods than men. But, finally, a barbarian, bolder than the rest, drew near to one of the old men, and putting forth a hand, gently stroked his long, white beard. Perhaps he had intended no harm; but the old Roman took it for an insult, and, raising the long staff which he carried in his hand, struck the Gaul a heavy blow over the head. At this the anger of the Gauls flamed up, and the old men were put to death, as they had expected when they prepared themselves for a sacrifice to the gods. The houses of the city were then robbed of the goods that had been left in them, and, fire having started, the streets and buildings were soon a mass of smouldering ashes.

But even then, the Gauls could not take the Capitol. The great rock was steep and well defended, and they soon found that they could not force their way to the top. They were obliged to settle down in the ruined city and besiege the Romans. This, however, was not the kind of fighting they were used to; they always found it tedious to sit still before an enemy and try to starve him into surrender. Indeed, in this case, there was some danger that they might starve themselves;

for they soon used up all the provisions that had been left in the town, and then, from day to day, they had to send out parts of their army to gather in food from the surrounding country.

On such a trip, one of these parties wandered as far as the town where Camillus was then living, in exile from his native city. Though he had been badly treated by the Romans, the general was grieved at the misfortunes that had come upon the town. Instead of planning for escape when the Gauls came into his neighborhood, he tried rather to punish them for what they had done to Rome; and, taking the young men of the city, he fell upon their camp by night and destroyed them utterly.

When the news of this act reached those Romans who had taken refuge in Veii, they began to recover from their terror, and to plan for the rescue of Rome. But first they must have a leader; and where, they asked, could they find a better one than Camillus, who had captured Veii for them, and had just shown them how to overcome the Gauls? Before Camillus could become their general, however, he had to be recalled from exile, and appointed to be their leader by the Senate. What was left of the Senate was besieged on the Capitol at Rome; so the men at Veii sent a youth to them, asking that they would recall Camillus and appoint him to command them.

This messenger boldly traveled the greater part of the way to Rome by day, but he waited until night to draw near to the city. Then he passed the river by swimming, with pieces of cork under his garments to hold him up, and approached the Capitol. Here, at a place which the Gauls had left unguarded, he managed to scramble up its rocky side, and gained the top in safety. He delivered his message to the Senate, and they granted his request gladly, and named Camillus, Dictator. Before morning the youth returned as he had come, bearing word back to Camillus and to the men at Veii.

The next day some of the Gauls at Rome found the marks of hands and feet where the messenger had climbed the side of the Capitol. Then they said to one another:

"Where it is easy for one man to get up, it will not be hard for many, one after another."

So the next night they made the attempt. Sending an unarmed man ahead to try the way, they followed in his steps, passing their weapons from one to another, and drawing each other up over the steep places. In this way, they reached the top, and reached it unnoticed by the Romans, for the sentinels were fast asleep, and even the dogs were quiet and gave no alarm.

But the sacred geese that were kept near the temple of Juno were more watchful. As the enemy approached their inclosure, they flapped their wings, cackling loudly, and this awoke an officer named Marcus Manlius, who was sleeping near by. At once, Manlius snatched up his arms, and, shouting to awake his comrades, he rushed to the spot where the first Gauls were just climbing over the wall of the citadel. One of them he slew with his sword, and another, at the same time, he struck full in the face with his shield, hurling him headlong from the rock; and this man, as he fell, threw down others who were below him. Then Manlius's companions joined him, and spears and stones fell thick and fast upon the climbing enemy, until the last of the attacking party was dashed to ruin at the foot of the rock, and the citadel was saved.

After this, the siege continued for many months, and it wore heavily on the Gauls and the Romans alike.

THE CAPITOL AT ROME.

At last both sides reached the limit of their endurance. It was that time of the year which was most unhealthy in Rome—the late summer and autumn—and many of the Gauls fell sick and died, for they were used to a colder and more healthful climate. The Romans were in a still worse condition, for their food was giving out. Even when Marcus Manlius had saved the Capitol, the citizens could do no kinder thing for him in return than to give him each half a pound of corn and half a pint of wine, taking this from the nourishment of their own bodies that he might be rewarded. Now there was not even this to give, and they had looked long and vainly for Camillus and the promised help from Veii. They were wearied with constant watching; and, weakened by hunger, they could scarcely bear the weight of their arms.

So, when the Gauls offered to break up the siege, and leave Rome in return for a thousand pounds of gold, the Romans were ready to consent. They brought out the gold for settlement; but, as the Gauls weighed it, the Romans charged them with balancing the scales unfairly. The only answer of the Gallic chief was to unbuckle his heavy sword from his waist, and throw it—belt, scabbard, and all—into the scale with the weights. The Romans indignantly demanded the meaning of this action.

"What should it mean but woe to the conquered?" he replied calmly.

And the Romans could do nothing but add the gold to make up the extra weight. They were conquered, indeed.

XV

Rebuilding the City.

THE stories go on to tell us that, before the Gauls got well away from Rome, Camillus arrived at last and defeated them, and took back the gold which had been given them as a ransom. It is likely, however, that this is only what the Romans wished could have happened, and not what really took place.

But, whether the Roman gold went with the Gauls or not, a very much heavier trouble had fallen upon the city, for the town was in ashes, and the people were scattered far and wide. It had taken hundreds of years to build Rome, and but a few months to destroy it. How the men and women must have mourned as they came back from their hiding-places and saw only heaps of stone and ashes where they had left their streets and homes! Only the Capitol lifted its head in the midst of the blackened ruins, bearing its buildings and temples unharmed.

Those who were in the greatest despair, as they gazed at the ruined town, were the common people. They had lost all of the little which they had possessed; and, as they looked at the ruins around the Capitol, they shrank from the task that they saw before them. Rome must be begun anew; and what toil it meant for them only to clear the ground and make ready for the work of building! And, after that was done, the greatest task would yet remain,—the gathering of the material and the construction of the dwellings.

Many of the people had returned from Veii, where they had been living in the well-built houses of that city, and they thought of them with regret.

"Why should we remain here, O Romans," cried the leaders of the people, "and toil at this great work? A home awaits us in Veii, ready built and with most fertile fields around it. That city was conquered by us from our enemies; let us make use of it now in our great need."

Then the people, looking at the ruins about them answered:

"Yes, let us go! Let us begin anew in Veii!"

But they did not go. When Camillus heard of the plans of the people, he went out among them, with the whole Senate following after him, and spoke to them long and earnestly.

"What is this that you think of doing, O Romans? Why have we struggled to recover our city from the Gauls, if we ourselves desert it as soon as it is recovered? Shall we now leave the Capitol, which the Romans and the gods still held, while the Gauls lay camped in the city? Shall even the citadel be deserted, now that the Gauls are fled and the Romans victorious? We possess a city founded by the gods; not a spot is there in it that is not full of them. Will you forsake them all by leaving Rome? Shall the Virgins forsake thee, O Vesta, and the priests of Rome become Veientians? Has our native soil so slight a hold on us, or this earth which we call mother? Does our love of country lie merely in the surface, and in the timber of our houses? For my part, I will confess to you, that, while I have been absent from my city, whenever it came into my thoughts, all these occurred to me,— the hills, the plains, the Tiber, the face of the country, so familiar to my eyes, and this sky, under which I have been born and educated. May these now, by your love of them, induce you to remain, rather than that they should cause you grief and regret after having left them. Not without good reason did gods and men choose this place for founding a city,—these most healthful hills, and this large river bearing the fruits of the inland country to us, and ours to the sea, —this place in the center of Italy.. The very size of our city before it was destroyed is a proof of its good situation. Where is the wisdom of your giving this up, now that you have proved it, to make trial of another city into which good fortune may not follow you? Here is the Capitol, which it was foretold should become the chief seat of empire. Here is the fire of Vesta. Here are the shields of Mars, let down from heaven. Here are all the gods, who will be favorable to you if you stay."

In spite of the speech of Camillus, however, the people still hesitated, and the senators even could not quite decide what it would be best for them to do. But, as they were still discussing the matter in the Senate house, an officer marched through the Forum with his soldiers, and called out:

"Standard-bearer, fix your standard. Let us halt here.'

His words reached the ears of the senators as they sat in anxious quiet, and it seemed to them like a message from the gods, commanding them to remain at Rome. They came out of the Senate-house, therefore, exclaiming that "they accepted the omen"; and the common people, when they were told of the occur-rence, allowed themselves to be persuaded to remain. Then the Senate ordered that Veii should be destroyed, so that the people might never again be tempted to leave Rome; and building materials were brought from the ruins there, and used in restoring the city. The Senate also gave the people liberty to take wood and stone free of charge, and to begin their houses wherever they could find a place. So, within a year, the city was rebuilt, after a fashion; but the houses at first were poor and mean, and the work was done so hurriedly that no attention was paid even to the course of the streets. The sewers, which had been

STANDARD BEARER.

laid in the old roadways, were now built over by private houses, and the new streets, winding in and out among the buildings, were very narrow and crooked.

The Romans were not allowed to rebuild their city

in peace, however. All the nations around them began to take advantage of their weakness to prevent them from growing strong and powerful once more. As we read the old stories, we wonder whether the Romans would have ever succeeded in restoring their city if it had not been for Camillus. He led them against their enemies many times, and always with success, often gaining the victory for them more by the enemy's fear of him than by the size of his armies or the strength of their arms.

At last, Camillus had grown to be an old man of eighty years, and when a call to battle came he feared that he was no longer fit to lead the Romans to victory. Nevertheless the citizens would not allow him to retire from the command; for his mind was still clear and strong, and they thought that this was worth more than youth and strength of body.

So Camillus went forth from Rome, with another man—Lucius Furius—for a companion in command; and he led his men cautiously to the seat of the war. The enemy had a larger force than Camillus, and were awaiting him in a city which had belonged to the Romans before the coming of the Gauls. When they saw the Romans approaching, they came out and offered to give battle immediately; for they thought that, by doing this, they would give Camillus less chance to plan his battle skilfully. But Camillus was too wise in the art of war to be caught in such a way, and he prepared to keep his men from battle until he saw a good chance for victory.

This made the enemy all the more eager, and they came close to the Roman camp and began digging trenches and preparing for battle as though daring them to fight. The Roman soldiers found this hard to bear, even though they were so few in number compared with the enemy. In their anger, they began to think that Camillus was holding them back more because of the weakness and fears of age, than from carefulness for their safety and final victory. The other general, the young Furius, was of this opinion also, and did not hesitate to say what he thought among the soldiers.

"Wars are the business of young men," he said, "and it ought to be so, for, in the best condition of the body, the mind is strongest also. Why should Camillus now hold his men quiet in the trenches when formerly he used to carry camps and cities at the first onset? What increase does he expect to his own strength; what falling off does he hope for in the enemy? Camillus has had a goodly share of years, as well as of glory. Shall we now allow the strength of the state to suffer because his body sinks into old age?"

When the soldiers, excited by these words, demanded battle, Furius appealed to the general.

"Camillus, we cannot withstand the violence of our soldiers, and the enemy insults us in a way not to be endured. Do you, who are but one man, yield to all, and allow us to do as we wish, that the victory may be ours the sooner."

Then the old general replied:

"Whatever wars have been fought, up to this day, under my single care, have not proved either my judgment or my good fortune to be wanting. But now I have a companion in my office of general, who is my equal in command and my superior in the vigor of youth. I have been accustomed to rule the violence of my army, not to be ruled by it. But with my companion's power I cannot interfere. You may do, Lucius Furius, that which you think best for the interest of Rome. I beg only one thing, and that is, that, in consideration of my years, I may not be placed in the front rank. Whatever duties of war an old man may discharge, in these I shall not be found wanting. And I pray the immortal gods that no misfortune may come upon the Romans to prove that my plan would have been the better one."

Then the Romans were drawn up in order of battle and advanced to the attack, leaving Camillus, as he had desired, with some reserve troops in the camp. The old general first posted strong guards about the camp, and then stood anxiously watching the advance of the Romans.

As he had feared, he did not see them gain a victory. At first, the enemy seemed to give way, and the Romans followed eagerly. But when the retreating soldiers had drawn them on to where the ground was difficult, they suddenly faced about; others of their men joined them, and they attacked the Romans at a disadvantage. It was not long before Camillus, from the high ground on which he watched the battle, saw the Roman line break and the soldiers come flying toward his camp.

Then Camillus commanded his men to lift him on his horse, and, calling to his troops, he led them out against the enemy. When he met the Romans rushing blindly back, he cried:

"Soldiers! is this the battle that you called for so eagerly? Why turn your faces toward the camp? Not a man of you shall my camp receive, except as victor! Having followed another leader, now follow Camillus, and conquer as you have done before."

At this the soldiers halted, stopped at first by shame. Then when they saw their old general, whom they had followed to so many conquests, go forward against the enemy in the front rank, they turned and joined him, with shouts and renewed courage. And once more Camillus led them on to victory.

It would have been natural after this for Camillus to have been angry with Lucius Furius, but he did not prove to be so. He seemed to wish to forget that it was the bad judgment of Furius which had brought on the battle, and to remember only that he had fought with the greatest bravery through it all.

"This day," said Camillus, "will be a lesson to him not to prefer his own plans to better ones."

So, when Camillus was appointed general for a new war soon after this, he chose this same Lucius Furius as his companion in command; and they went out together, once more, in friendliness and good fellowship. This seems indeed a different Camillus from the one who had been exiled because he could not live without quarreling with his fellow citizens. Now you find him, instead of urging matters of dispute, forgiving a real injury, and showing only kindness to the man who had scorned him in his old age. He had learned something nobler, during his long life, than how to conduct a war successfully; for at the last, he was willing to return good for evil, and to make a friend of one who might have been his enemy.

Camillus lived for some years longer, and when he died the people felt as though they had lost a second Romulus; for he had almost founded their city a second time, by persuading them to remain in it after the retreat of the Gauls, and by protecting them from their enemies while they rebuilt their dwellings. The wisdom of his desire to remain at Rome was seen even before his death, for the city had already sprung up in a vigorous new growth; and we now believe, as Camillus did then, that nowhere else could Rome have grown to be the great city which it finally became.

XVI

The New Rome.

THE labor and self-denial of these first years of the new city were hard for its people to endure, and yet they had to carry the burden alone. If Rome had been a modern town overcome by misfortune, its inhabitants would have received generous aid from all the country round. In our time, whether it has been at the Chicago fire, the Charleston earthquake, or the Galveston flood, money, food, and clothing have poured upon the sufferers from every side. The neighbors of ancient Rome, however, would have preferred to injure, rather than to aid, the people of the destroyed city. It was only owing to the wisdom and skill of Camillus, and the determination of her own people that Rome at length recovered from her disaster, and became a powerful city once more.

In one way their troubles were a good thing for the Romans. The patricians found it so important, for their own good, that the common people should stay at Rome and help in the work of rebuilding the city, that they became willing to give up many of the rights which, before this, they had kept to themselves. It was not many years after the new Rome had been built that a man from the plebeians was elected consul, along with a man of noble birth. This was a great victory for the common people, and it was soon followed by others. Before a century had passed from the coming of the Gauls, the plebeians were allowed to hold any office to which a patrician could be elected, and the old distinctions between the classes were entirely removed.

In spite of the fact that Camillus had called their hills "most healthful," Rome was troubled for many years after the rebuilding of the city with illness among the people. You will remember that the Gauls sickened quickly in Rome; and now, even the citizens themselves, who were used to the climate, died in great numbers. This indeed was the cause of the death of Camillus himself, after all his long years of fighting on Roman battlefields; and sometimes there was so much illness among the people that the armies could not be sent out against their enemies as usual.

This trouble was due partly to a lack of good water in the city. The well water about Rome, and also the water of the Tiber, was impure; and the cisterns did not furnish enough for the use of the people. The Romans must have felt this need very keenly, for, while they were fighting battles on every side, they set themselves to work to bring in a good supply of water from outside the city, as is now done in all of our large towns. Eight miles from Rome there were hills where pure water could be found in plenty, and they brought this into the city in a passage which they built for it under ground.

Such a passage for water they called an "aqueduct," and we still use the same word ourselves, having received it from the Romans. We have usually built our aqueducts above ground, however, while the

Romans did not dare do this at first for fear their enemies might succeed in turning the stream aside, and thus leave the city without water. But as Rome

RUINS OF A ROMAN AQUEDUCT.

conquered the people about her, and the city grew larger and needed a greater supply, many new aqueducts were built, which were placed above the ground. Even yet you can see, near Rome, the remains of some of the great stone troughs—sometimes built high up in the air on arches—in which water was brought many miles from the pure sources in the hills.

At this time, also, the Romans began a work which was as great as the building of their aqueducts,—the making of good roads. As soon as they had begun to send out armies to fight with the neighboring cities, they must have seen the need of well-built roads that could be used through all the seasons of the year, and in wet and dry weather alike. Such roads became still more necessary now that they had come to rule lands and cities lying many miles from home. So while the citizens were bringing good water into Rome, they began their first long road; and the man who led them in building their aqueduct was foremost in making this also. His name was Appius Claudius, and he was quite as great a man as any of the Roman generals that we are told so much about. Because the road was built under his direction, the Romans called it the "Appian Way," and to-day what remains of it is still known by this name.

From the beginning, the Romans built their roads with the greatest care. First, after they had removed the earth to the proper depth, they placed a layer of large flat stones on the ground. Then a layer, nine inches thick, of smaller stones, was laid upon these, and cemented together with lime. Next came a layer, about six inches thick, of still smaller stones, and this too was bound together with cement. At last, on top of all, blocks of very hard stone were laid, and fitted closely together, so as to make a perfectly smooth surface whether for walking or driving. Is it any wonder that roads built with such care have lasted for two thousand years?

This building of roads and bringing of water into the city was not a small thing for the Romans to do, as perhaps it may seem now, when well-paved streets and waterworks are to be found in every large town. The Romans did this when such things were only beginning to be thought of by men, and they did it so well that they set an example which the whole world

A ROMAN ROAD.

has been glad to follow ever since. They saw what they needed, then they thought out the best way to meet their wants; and, last of all, they were willing to work long and hard in order to do well whatever they undertook. It is this as much as anything else which made the Romans become one of the greatest nations that the world has ever seen. They thought well and worked hard, whether it was in fighting battles or building roads, and in the end this made them the masters of the world.

The Romans not only thought things out for them-selves, however; they were always ready to learn from others.   Whatever they saw that seemed good to them, they borrowed and made part of themselves.   They learned from their neighbors to the north a great deal of that knowledge of building which they used in con-structing their temples and aqueducts.   When, for the first time, they went to war with a foe beyond the sea, they taught themselves how to build war-vessels from a ship of the enemy which was wrecked on their shores. When they found that the short, straight sword, which the people of Spain used, was better than their own, they armed their soldiers with that.   And when they discovered that the Greeks were greater poets and artists than they were, they took them to be their teachers in art and literature.

But, besides the power of the Romans to think, to work, and to learn from others, there was something else that made their city strong.   This was the love and devotion of her people.   The best of the Romans were willing to die for her, and did die for her, not only by going into battle and laying down their lives there, but in other ways as well.

Old writers tell us that once a great chasm, many feet deep, suddenly opened in the Forum.   This must have been caused by an earthquake, such as those which still often occur in Italy, and more rarely in our own land.   The Romans were greatly distressed by this opening, and they tried to fill it by throwing earth into it.   But, in spite of all their efforts, they could make no headway.   Then they could only look upon it as a work of the gods, and they asked the priests how it might be closed once more. The priests replied:

"Search out what is the most precious thing of the Roman people, for that is what must be thrown into the chasm in order to satisfy the gods and make sure that the city will last forever."

As they considered among themselves what this "most precious thing of the Roman people" might be, Marcus Curtius, a youth who had done great deeds in war, came forward.

"Can you doubt what this means?" he exclaimed. "Is there any greater good for Romans than arms and bravery? This is what the gods demand; and I will devote myself as a sacrifice to them, so that my country may never perish."

He put on his richest armor and, mounting his horse, rode to the edge of the chasm, while the people of Rome crowded the Forum and stood watching. When he had prayed to the gods, Curtius leaped his horse into the opening, and horse and rider disappeared from sight. After that the chasm closed, and all that was left to show where the opening had been was a little pool of water, which the Romans named the Curtian lake, in honor of the youth who had so willingly offered himself for the good of his city.

At another time, a Roman named Decius Mus sacrificed himself in the same unselfish spirit. Decius was consul, and was leading the army in battle when he saw that the Romans were giving way and the enemy was pressing on to victory.

"Valerius," he cried, to the chief priest who stood by him, "we have need of the aid of the gods. Come!

tell me the words by which I may offer myself a sacrifice for my soldiers.''

Then, with his head covered and leaning on a spear, he repeated these words after the priest:

"Janus, Jupiter, Father Mars, and all ye gods under whose power we and our enemies are: I pray you that you will grant strength to the Roman people, that they may strike the enemies of the Romans with terror, dismay, and death. I devote the soldiers of the enemy together with myself to the gods of the dead, for the sake of the soldiers of Rome.''

He then mounted his horse, and rushed into the midst of the enemy, where he fell pierced by many weapons. The Roman soldiers, who followed him in his attack, were victorious; but they freely gave the honor of their success to the man who had offered himself as a sacrifice for his army.

XVII

The War with Pyrrhus.

THE curving range of the Apennines divides **Italy** into three distinct parts,—the valley of the **Po,** the longer western slope and the plains about the southern gulf. Within a hundred years after the attack of the Gauls the Romans ruled all the lands around them between the mountains and the sea. But they had not yet crossed the Apennines to the north; nor had they thought of going beyond them in the south, until something happened there which forced them to do so.

The southern coast of Italy was not occupied by Italians, but by Greeks, who had come across the sea a long time before, and built cities on the southern shores of the peninsula, and on the island of Sicily. They were a gay, fickle people, who had grown to be much less worthy in character than the old Greeks who had fought the Persians so well in former days. They preferred to hire soldiers to fight for them, instead of doing it themselves; for they loved the bustle and chatter of their city life, and the amusement of their open-air theaters, too much to exchange them willingly for the dangers of the battlefield.

The most important of these Greek cities in Italy was Tarentum, which lay on the western side of the heel of the peninsula. There the people had built their theater in a place which overlooked the sea; and as they were gathered here one day, they saw ten Roman war vessels approaching the city harbor. Now there was an agreement between the Romans and the people of Tarentum that the Roman war ships should not sail beyond a certain point on the southern shore, so when the Tarentines saw these vessels coming in close to their town they were very angry. They did not stop to think that the Romans might be coming peacefully, and with no thought of harm. They rushed headlong from the theater to the shore, boarded their ships and rowed out to attack the Roman vessels. As the Romans were entirely unprepared for battle, five of their ships were sunk, and the men were taken prisoners.

The other five ships managed to escape, and when they returned to Rome with the news of how they had been treated the Romans were very indignant. But they did not want to go to war with the people of Tarentum; so, instead of preparing an army to attack the city, they sent ambassadors to demand an explanation of the wrong that had been done them.

When these ambassadors reached Tarentum, they were led before a large body of the citizens, in order that they might state their business in the hearing of all. Their grave manner and broken speech, as they tried to make their meaning clear in the Greek tongue, amused the Tarentines immensely. They laughed at them and mocked their blunders, and, at last, one wretched fellow threw dirt on the clean white toga of one of the ambassadors.

At this, the Greeks laughed louder than ever; but

the insulted Roman raised the soiled folds of his gown and held them before the eyes of the people.

"Laugh on," he cried; "but this stain can only be washed out with blood."

Then the ambassadors departed, and the two cities began to prepare for war,—but in what different ways! The Romans gathered their men together as usual, and sent them under the command of a consul across the mountains into southern Italy. The Tarentines meanwhile went over into Greece, seeking a general there who could bring an army to fight for them against the Romans.

There were many men in the Grecian peninsula at this time who were willing enough to fight, and who knew how to fight well; but the man to whom the Tarentines sent was especially ready to give the help that they asked. This was Pyrrhus, the king of one of the little countries of western Greece,—a brave and generous man, and one of the best soldiers of that time. He was related to Alexander the Great, who a few years before this had become the conqueror of Greece and of much of the world besides. From his boyhood Pyrrhus had lived with the Greek armies at home, in Asia, and in Egypt; and he had determined that if he should ever have the chance he would try to become, like Alexander, a conqueror of great nations. So now, when the Tarentines sent to him and begged his help against the Romans, he readily gave his consent, and began to plan victories for himself in the west as great as those which Alexander had won in the east. For he meant not only to help the Tarentines against Rome, but to bring all the Greek cities of Italy and of the island of Sicily under his rule at the same time.

When Pyrrhus had gathered his army together and sailed to Tarentum, the foolish people of that city suddenly discovered that they had given themselves a stern ruler where they had only asked help against their enemy. The king had no patience with their lightness and gayety in such a time of danger. He closed their theater and public meeting-places, and set the people to work helping his soldiers in their task of preparing for the Romans. The Tarentines obeyed unwillingly; perhaps they were already beginning to wish that they had not been so rash in making trouble, or so ready to ask aid when the trouble had come.

Soon after Pyrrhus reached Italy, the two armies— the Greek and the Roman—met in battle near Tarentum. On both sides, the men fought so bravely that for a time it could not be told which would gain the victory. The Greeks formed their men in one solid mass, drawn close together with their shields touching and their great spears, eighteen feet long, extending far out in front of them. The Romans grouped theirs in many small companies, which were arranged loosely into three ranks, one behind the other; in this way each company and each rank could act separately, while all supported one another. The Greeks were the strongest in defending themselves on a level surface, for the Romans could scarcely break through the dense hedge of their spear-points, and get near enough to reach them with their short swords. But the Romans could attack their enemies more freely than the Greeks, and could move more easily over rough ground.

In this battle, the Romans rushed time and again at the solid ranks of the Greeks, and seemed determined never to give up the effort to break through and throw them into disorder. But Pyrrhus had with him in his army something of which the Romans had never seen the like before. This was a herd of elephants; and when these huge beasts charged upon the army, with towers on their backs full of armed men, the Romans faltered in dismay. Their horses went mad with fright and, whirling about, trampled down their own masters. Then the Romans retreated in confusion, and the battle was lost.

A ROMAN SOLDIER.

Pyrrhus had gained the first victory, but he saw that he had met enemies who could not be despised, even though they had been defeated. When the fight was over, he stood upon the battlefield and saw the Roman dead all lying with their faces turned toward the enemy.

"If these were my soldiers," he said, "and I were their general, I could surely conquer the world."

After this battle, Pyrrhus sent his trusted friend Cineas to Rome to propose terms of peace to the Senate, for he thought that the Romans would now be ready to give up the war. Cineas was as great as a statesman as Pyrrhus was as a general, and it was said of him that his tongue had taken more cities for his master than Pyrrhus had taken with his armies. During his visit to Rome, he made himself most agreeable to the citizens. He had such a good memory that after one day he could call every great man by his name, and he was such a good judge of men that he never failed to treat each person in the way that would be most pleasing to him. So all the Romans liked him, though he was their enemy; and the Senate was almost persuaded by him to do as Pyrrhus wished, and settle upon a peace.

But there was one person in Rome whom Cineas could not win over. This was Appius Claudius, who had constructed the first aqueduct, and had built the Appian Way. He was now an old man, gray-haired and blind, and it had been a long time since he had gone from his home to take his place in the Senate. But when he heard that peace was about to be made with Pyrrhus, he commanded his servants to take him up and carry him in his chair through the Forum to the Senate house. There his sons and sons-in-law met him at the door, and when he was led in and rose to speak, he was received with a respectful silence.

"Until this time, O senators," he said, "I have borne the misfortune of my blindness with some impatience. But now, when I hear this dishonorable purpose of yours, it is my great sorrow that, being blind, I am not deaf also. To make peace with Pyrrhus will be to destroy the glory of Rome. Do not persuade yourselves that making a friend of Pyrrhus is the way to send him back to his country. It is the way, rather, to show the world that you can be conquered in one battle; and soon other invaders will be upon us. The true way to rid us of our dangers is for Rome never to treat with a foreign enemy while his army remains in Italy."

The senators were shamed by the noble courage of the aged Claudius. Instead of making peace with Pyrrhus, they sent Cineas back to his master with the message that they would not treat with him about terms of peace and friendship until his army was removed from Italian soil; and they added that, so long as he stayed in Italy under arms, they would continue to fight with him, even though he should defeat them many times.

This firm answer made a deep impression upon Cineas. When he returned to Pyrrhus and the king asked him what he thought of the Romans and their government, he answered:

"The Roman Senate, Sire, is an assembly of kings."

Pyrrhus himself soon had a chance to test the spirit of one of the Romans of that day. The Senate sent Caius Fabricius to the king, shortly after this, to treat for the return of the Roman prisoners who had been taken by the Greeks. Cineas told Pyrrhus that Fabricius was one who stood very high among the Romans, as an honest man and a good soldier, but that he was very poor. So Pyrrhus received him with kindness, and tried to bribe him with gold. But Fabricius refused to accept the king's gifts.

"If I am dishonest," said he, "how can I be worth a bribe? And if I am honest, how can you expect me to take one?"

Then Pyrrhus tried him in another way. The next

day he commanded that one of the largest of the elephants should be placed behind the curtains while he and Fabricius sat talking together. At a signal from the king, the curtains were drawn aside, and the elephant, raising his trunk just over the head of Fabricius, trumpeted loudly. But the Roman only turned quietly, and said to Pyrrhus:

"Neither your money yesterday, O King, nor this beast to-day, can move me."

Pyrrhus himself was noble enough of soul to admire Fabricius greatly. To show his favor to him, he allowed him to take the Roman prisoners with him when he returned to Rome; for a great festival in honor of the god Saturn was about to be celebrated, and all Romans wished to take part in it. Fabricius, for his part, gave a promise to the king that if the Senate did not agree to make peace, the men should all come back to him when the holiday was past.

This festival to Saturn was held each year in the latter part of December, and was a sort of Thanksgiving holiday. It was a time when the Romans gave presents, as we do now at Christmas, and the poor people received gifts of oil and wine, while the servants of the wealthy carried baskets of nuts, figs, and apples to their masters' friends. In this happy, joyous season, the boys all had new tunics and new shoes, and the slaves were allowed to be equal to their masters for once in the long year.

The holiday must have passed only too quickly for the prisoners of Pyrrhus; for the Roman Senate again refused to agree to a peace, and they were sent back to the Greeks as soon as the festival was over. The senators were so anxious to keep the promise of Fabricius unbroken, that they commanded that any prisoner who remained behind should be put to death; but this order was not needed, for they all returned faithfully to their captivity.

It was not long after this that the Romans and the Greeks met in battle a second time. Once more the Romans were defeated; but they fought as stubbornly as they had in the first battle, and again it was only the elephants that won the victory for Pyrrhus. After the battle, one of the friends of the king came to him and wished him joy over his victory. But Pyrrhus replied, seeing the large number of his own men who had fallen: "One more such victory as this, and I am lost."

The king was thinking how far he was from the country of his own brave soldiers; and how difficult it would be to fill up the vacant places in his army with men who were as good as those he had lost, for even Pyrrhus could not make warriors out of the Greeks of Italy. His situation was very different therefore from that of the Romans. Among them every man was a soldier, and as soon as one army was destroyed, another as large and well-trained could be raised to take its place.

So after this second battle, Pyrrhus did not care to fight again with the Romans. He left Italy and went over to the island of Sicily, and tried to make himself master of the cities there. He remained away for three years, and when he returned to Italy, he found that the Romans had made good use of his absence. They had gained all the southern part of the peninsula except the city of Tarentum, and they were now in better condition to give battle to him than ever.

The Romans had seen that the close ranks of the Greeks fought best upon a level surface; so, when a third battle with Pyrrhus took place, they placed themselves on rough, uneven ground. The soldiers had also lost much of their fear of the elephants by this time; and, when the great beasts charged at them in this battle, they hurled darts and spears at them, and so wounded and vexed the animals that at last they turned and rushed back upon the Greeks themselves. In this way the solid mass of Pyrrhus's soldiers was broken up, and after that it was not long until his whole army was terribly defeated.

After this third battle, Pyrrhus was obliged to leave Italy and go back to his own country, a disappointed man. He had failed to conquer an empire in the west, as he had planned; and the Romans, with their power for enduring defeat, had been the cause of his failure. Not long after he had gone, the city of Tarentum itself fell into the hands of the Romans; and this left them masters of the entire peninsula south of the valley of the Po.

XVIII

Rome and the Carthaginians.

NOW that the Romans had become masters of almost the whole of the peninsula of Italy, you might expect that their wars would cease, and that they would be left to govern peaceably what their arms had won. Instead of this they had soon to prepare for a struggle which was to prove the longest and hardest that they ever experienced. This was due to the fact that just across the Mediterranean Sea from Italy, there was another people who had also been able to make themselves rulers over other lands and nations; and, after the Romans had conquered the Greeks of southern Italy, there was no longer any barrier standing between these two powerful states.

This nation had founded the city of Carthage more than a hundred years before Romulus began the first settlement on the Palatine hill; and it had now become a larger and richer city than Rome. Its people ruled a great part of the coast of Africa, Spain, and Sicily, and most of the islands of the western Mediterranean.

The people of Carthage were Phœnicians, and their mother country was along the eastern shores of the Mediterranean. They were of the same race as the Jews, who dwelt near by the mother land in Palestine; and they were more foreign in speech and religion

than any other people with whom the Romans had
come in contact. They were a nation of sailors and
traders and their ships were the best then known to
men. They were the first to discover that they could
steer their vessels through boundless waters by using
the North Star to guide them; so, while other nations
still kept safely in sight of the shores of the Mediterranean in their voyaging, the Phœnicians pushed
boldly out into the broad Atlantic, and sailed as far as
the island of Great Britain on the north, and some
distance south down the coast of Africa. They were
the explorers of that long-ago time; and moreover,
like the nations of later days, they made settlements
wherever they could find a good harbor, with a fertile
country around it, or with mines of tin or precious
metals. And they did more, even, than this. In
order to keep their records and accounts, they invented
the alphabet which we use to-day; and taught these
letters to the Greeks and the Romans, who made use
of them in writing their different languages.

So, when the Phœnicians left their old home to
found a new city in the west, they brought with them
much useful knowledge. Their children, too, and
their children's children, made good use of their
inherited wisdom. By the time the Romans had conquered southern Italy, their city of Carthage was said
to cover twenty-three miles of country; and the sails
of its ships dotted the waters of the western Mediterranean. The Carthaginians were good builders, also,
as well as good sailors and traders. They had protected their city on the land side by three great walls,
one inside of the other, and these walls were far

stronger and better built than those which surrounded Rome. The space between the walls was taken up with stables for the elephants and war horses, and here were kept three hundred of the one and four thousand of the other. To shelter their great fleet two large harbors had been dug, in addition to the natural bay on which the city was built,—one for the trading vessels, and one for the ships of war.

The Carthaginians were a powerful nation and very jealous of their power, being determined to prevent any other people from sharing in it. They regarded the sea, on which their many vessels came and went, as belonging to themselves alone; and when they found the ships of other nations sailing in their waters, they did not hesitate to capture the vessels and to drown the men that they found on them. They are said to have boasted once that, without their permission, the Romans could not even wash their hands in the waters of the sea.

The struggle between the Romans and the Carthaginians began in Sicily. The Carthaginians had long had possession of the western part of the island, while the eastern part was ruled by a number of Greek cities. It was to take the part of these cities against the Carthaginians that Pyrrhus had gone to Sicily; so the Carthaginians were friendly to Rome until the Romans had driven Pyrrhus back to his eastern home. As soon as he was disposed of, however, the friendship between Rome and Carthage began to cool. Pyrrhus had foreseen that this would be so; and as he had left the island of Sicily he had looked back at its shores and exclaimed:

What a field we are leaving for the Romans and the Carthaginians to contend upon!"

Directly across the strait which separates Italy from Sicily, was a Greek city which soon after this got into very serious trouble with one of its neighbors. The people in the city were divided as to what they should do for help; so one party sent to Rome for aid, while the other called upon the Carthaginians. Now, the Romans could not permit the Carthaginians to gain a foothold so near to Italy as this and, rather against their will, they felt obliged to send the aid which had been asked. The result was the first war between Rome and Carthage.

Although the Carthaginians were masters of the sea, they were not prepared to fight the Romans on land. They had no army of citizens to depend on, such as Rome possessed. They hired their soldiers, as you will remember the Tarentines did, and gathered them together from many different countries. So it took them a long time to get a strong army ready to fight in Sicily; and in the meantime the Romans won the first victories and took important towns from them.

But the Romans soon discovered that they could make few lasting gains in fighting against the Carthaginians, without a navy to help them. They might conquer all Sicily with their armies, but when the war vessels of the Carthaginians came sailing around the island, the cities on the coast which had given themselves to the Romans would have to go back to the Carthaginian side once more. Besides this, the ships of Carthage could dash in from the sea upon the coast of Italy, and destroy a city or ruin a whole stretch of country before the Italians could make a move to defend themselves. Meanwhile the Romans did not seem to be able to get at their enemies to do them any serious harm, for they had few war vessels and little experience in using those they had.

When the Romans realized this, they did one of the most daring things that we read of in their history. They determined to build a fleet, and go out and meet the Carthaginians on the sea, where they had so long been masters. They took for their model a Carthaginian ship that had been wrecked on their shores, and within sixty days, the old writers say, a growing wood was changed into a fleet of one hundred and twenty ships.

While the vessels were building, they had also to find rowers for their new fleet, and to train them for their work. To do this, tiers of seats, arranged one above the other, like the benches of rowers in a ship were built upon the ground; and on these the men took their places daily, and were taught to move their great oars all together, in obedience to the voice of the rowing master. Then, when the ships were done, the men were given a short time to practice on the water the movements which they had learned on the land; and after that the fleet sailed away to Sicily to seek out and fight their enemies.

But for all their bold and determined spirit, the Romans knew very well that they could not, for some time, hope to be a match for the skilful Carthaginian sailors. Their hastily-made ships were clumsy and hard to manage, and the green wood of which they were built was already beginning to warp apart and let in the water.   Their rowers and sailing-masters did not know how to make the best even of the poor ships they had; and for knowledge of the sea itself— its storms and currents, and the harbors of its coasts —they had to depend upon people of other cities, whom they hired to help them.   The only way that

NAVAL BATTLE.

the Romans could hope to win a sea-fight was by getting their vessels right alongside the ships of the enemy, and then fighting it out with their spears and swords, just as they would a battle on the land.

To enable their vessels to do this, some clever man thought out a plan which was adopted on all the ships. A strong mast was planted in the prow of every Roman vessel, and at the base of this was fastened a long plank or platform, in such a way that the outer end could be pulled up and let down, like the drawbridge of a castle, in front or on either side of the vessel. At the end of the plank, and pointing downward, a long spike was fixed, so that when the plank was let fall on the deck of the enemy's ship this spike would sink deep into the wood and hold it fast. When the platform was raised against the mast, this sharp piece of iron sticking out in front looked so much like the bill of some great bird that the Romans gave the name of "crow" to the contrivance.

When the Carthaginians saw the Roman ships sailing up to meet them, they were puzzled at first by the strange structures in their bows; but they knew that the Romans were ignorant of everything that had to do with managing ships, so they supposed that it was some clumsy device of no importance. They rowed straight out to meet them, therefore, and sought to ram their vessels with the prows of their own ships. But no sooner did a Carthaginian vessel come within reach of a Roman than down fell the "crow" of the latter, and the two ships were held firmly together. Then Roman soldiers poured across the bridge thus made, and fought upon the deck as if on land. In this way they captured or destroyed fifty of the Carthaginian ships, and those that were left were glad enough to find safety in flight from the terrible Roman "crows."

This was the first Roman victory on the sea, but many others followed it. Now that they had a fleet, moreover, the Romans could take an army across the sea to Africa, and there fight the Carthaginians in their own land. This they did, and the Roman general, Regulus, was very successful for a time, pushing the Carthaginians so hard that they were forced at last to ask for peace.

Then Regulus showed how little he knew the brave people with whom he was fighting. He seemed to think that Carthage was as completely conquered as the little Italian towns which Rome had been taking, one by one, for so many years. The terms of peace which he offered were so hard that the Carthaginians concluded that they could not be left in a worse condition even if Carthage itself was captured, so they resolved to continue the war. Fortunately for them, the Carthaginians now found a good general, who knew how to use their cavalry and their elephants. Soon Regulus himself was defeated and taken prisoner; and for five years he was kept a captive at Carthage, while the war continued on land and sea.

It had been thirteen years since the Romans had first crossed over into Sicily, when ambassadors came again from Carthage to treat for peace. According to the old stories Regulus was now taken from his prison and sent to Rome, along with the Carthaginian ambassadors, to assist them in their purpose; and he was obliged to promise that if peace was not made he would return at once to Carthage.

The Carthaginians sent Regulus with their ambassadors because they thought that, for his own sake, he would do all that he could to help bring the war to a close. But when he reached Rome, he was noble enough to forget himself in his love for his country.

He advised the Senate not to make peace, and not to exchange their Carthaginian prisoners for the Romans who were held at Carthage.

"Let not the Senate buy with gold what ought to be won back only by force of arms; and let those Romans who surrendered when they ought to have died in battle, die at last in the land that saw their disgrace."

When Regulus said this, he knew that if he returned after such a speech, the Carthaginians would put him to death. For a while the Senate hesitated, out of pity for him; but at last the peace which had been asked was refused. Then Regulus went quietly back to Carthage, as he had promised; and if we may believe the story, met a cruel death at the hands of his disappointed enemies.

For ten years longer, the war dragged on, until at last neither Carthage nor Rome had money or men to spend in further efforts. Rome had been most unfortunate at sea. Fleet after fleet which she sent to Sicily and Africa was wrecked and destroyed by the terrible storms which rage there at certain seasons of the year and which the Romans were not experienced enough to guard against.

After this had happened several times, the people determined to make one more effort. Their ships were all gone, and there was no money in the treasury to build new ones; but the wealthy citizens of Rome joined together and built a fleet of two hundred vessels at their own expense. They only asked, in return, that if the city could ever repay them, it would do so.

With this fleet the Romans again set out, and this time they were as successful as in their first venture upon the sea. They had now learned from their mistakes and misfortunes, while the Carthaginians had become careless; so, when the Romans came up with the Carthaginian fleet off the western coast of Sicily, they sunk fifty of the enemy's vessels and captured seventy more.

Then Carthage and Rome made peace, for they were too well matched at the time for either city to be entirely conquered. Carthage had suffered most in this first war; so she was obliged to give up all claim to Sicily, to release the Roman prisoners without a ransom, and besides this, to pay a large sum of money for the expenses of the war. Rome took possession of the part of Sicily which the Carthaginians had held, and set up a government over it. Before many years had gone by, the whole island passed under Roman control, and became the city's first possession outside of Italy.

XIX

The War with Hannibal.

AFTER the Carthaginians had made peace with Rome, and had withdrawn their troops from Sicily, they had to endure three terrible years of warfare with their own subjects and soldiers, in the country round about Carthage. But through all this time of defeat and disaster, there was one man among them who remained undismayed.

This was Hamilcar, the greatest of their generals and at that time the only man among the Carthaginians whom the Romans feared. Hamilcar had fought Rome successfully, as long as his city could give him money and men to fight with; and when he saw that Carthage could do no more, it was he who had made the peace. He had no thought of a lasting peace with Rome, however; he hated that city as much as he loved Carthage, and he was already planning a way to injure her, while he made up to his own country for the loss of Sicily. Both of these objects he thought he could gain by conquering the Spanish peninsula, where the Carthaginians had already made settlements; and when he brought the matter before the Senate at Carthage, they gave him permission to take an army there and see what he could do.

As Hamilcar was preparing to leave for Spain with

his army, he went before the altar of one of the Carthaginian gods, and offered sacrifice for the success of his plans. During the ceremony, his little son Hannibal, who was then about nine years old, stood beside him; and when it was over, Hamilcar turned to the boy and asked if he would like to go with him to Spain. When the lad eagerly answered that he should like very much to do so, Hamilcar took him by the hand and led him to the altar.

"Then lay your hand upon the sacrifice," he commanded, "and swear that you will never be friends with Rome, so long as you shall live."

The boy did as he was bidden; and in due time he was taken away to Spain, with the thought deep in his breast that he was now the enemy of Rome forever. From that time, he grew up in the camp of his father, and his daily lessons were in the arts of war and of generalship. He was Hamilcar's companion while he conquered the rich peninsula of Spain for Carthage; and before his father had died, Hannibal had learned all that he could teach him of warfare and of government.

After Hamilcar was gone, Hannibal proved himself a worthy son of so great a parent, and when he was only twenty-seven years of age, he was chosen to fill his father's place as commander of the Carthaginian army. This army was made up, in large part, of men from the conquered nations in Spain; but under the leadership of Hannibal, it did not matter much who the soldiers were that formed the army. His men became simply the soldiers of Hannibal, and were so filled with love and admiration for their general, that they were ready to follow him anywhere and do anything that he commanded.

When Hannibal had got his army in good condition, he attacked a town in Spain that was friendly to Rome, and conquered it. The Roman Senate was already beginning to fear this son of Hamilcar as it had feared Hamilcar himself, and when news came of the attack on this friendly town, it sent ambassadors to Carthage to demand that Hannibal should be given up to the Romans. But the Carthaginians would not consent to this. Then the leader of the Roman ambassadors gathered up the folds of his toga and held them before him, saying:

"I carry here peace and war; which shall I give to you?"

"You may give us whichever you choose," replied the Carthaginians.

"Then I give you war," cried the Roman, as he shook out the folds of his toga.

In this way, the second war between Rome and Carthage was declared. But it was not really a struggle between the two states which now began. It was rather a conflict between all the power of Rome, on the one side, and Hannibal, with his devoted army and his vow of hatred to the Romans, on the other. When Hannibal heard in Spain that war had been declared, he was prepared for it, and needed only to consider how he might attack his enemies.

He was determined that this war should be fought on Roman, and not on Carthaginian, ground; in Italy, instead of Africa. With this settled upon he had the choice of two ways of reaching Italy from Spain. He might cross the sea in Carthaginian ships, or he might go by land, through Spain and Gaul. If he chose the latter way, he would have to make a long march through an unfriendly country, and cross the forbidding barrier of the Alps. If he chose to go by sea, he ran the risk of wreck by storms, and defeat and capture by the Roman fleet, which was now stronger

HANNIBAL.

than that of the Carthaginians. Either way, it was a choice of evils.

Hannibal decided to go by land; but we may be sure of one thing,—that he did not know quite how difficult a path it was that he had chosen. He was the greatest man of his time, but he had no good way of learning the simple facts about the world he lived in which you are taught in every day's geography lesson. The thought of the mountains to be climbed, and the rivers to be crossed, in the long journey, did not make him hesitate, for he did not fully know them. He knew that the Gauls had passed through the high Alps, —then why might not he do it also? He could have had no clear idea even of the distance his soldiers would have to march before they reached Italy; for his guides at any place could tell him the way and the distances for only a few days' march ahead, and when that was passed he would have to find other persons who knew the country beyond, and would undertake to guide his army on.

It was in the month of April that Hannibal started on his long march. Besides the many thousand men, both infantry and cavalry, who made up his army, he took with him thirty-seven of the Carthaginian elephants to use in battle, and many horses and mules to carry the baggage of the army.

As soon as he got out of the territory that had been conquered by Carthage, his troubles began. He had to fight his way against unfriendly natives through northern Spain; and it was midsummer before he had crossed the mountains which separate the peninsula from Gaul. Then, in a short time, he came to the swiftly flowing Rhone, where the Gauls gathered on the opposite bank, and tried to prevent him from crossing. Hannibal soon overcame these enemies, however, and led his army safely over in canoes and boats, which his men collected along the river; but the elephants could only be taken across after he had prepared great rafts on which to ferry them.

After they had passed the Rhone, the way was easy until they came to the foot of the Alps; but there the greatest difficulties of the march began.   The way now lay along steep, narrow paths, up which the horses and elephants could scarcely climb; and often a single slip or misstep would have been enough to send them rolling and tumbling a thousand feet down the mountain side, to be dashed to pieces on the rocks below.   The people who inhabited the mountains, too, were unfriendly to the Carthaginians.   They stationed themselves on either side of the zigzag path up which the army toiled, and hurled stones and weapons upon them from the heights above.   These threw the long line of baggage animals into great disorder, and the wounded and frightened horses galloped back and forth, and either fell themselves or crowded others off over the cliffs and down the mountain side, carrying with them as they fell baggage which the army could ill afford to lose.   Again and again Hannibal was obliged to take some of his best men and clamber up the cliffs and over the rocks to attack and drive off these enemies; and once in such an attempt he and his men were separated from the rest of the army, and were forced to remain on their guard all night long, under the shelter of a great white rock which stood by the side of the path.

At last, on the ninth day after they had begun their ascent, the army reached the summit of the pass. After that they were no longer troubled by attacks from the mountain tribes.   Here Hannibal remained for two days, in order to rest his men and beasts; and while they tarried there, many of the horses which

had taken fright and run away, and many of the beasts
of burden, which had gotten rid of their loads, came
straggling into camp, having followed the tracks of the
army.

After they had rested sufficiently, they began the
descent into Italy, and then new difficulties presented
themselves. The way was down-hill, to be sure, but
the slope was more abrupt than on the other side of
the mountains. It was now late in the autumn, moreover; and as the cold comes early in these high regions,
the paths were already covered with a thin coating of
new-fallen snow, which caused the men and beasts to
slip, and made the descent more dangerous than the
ascent had been. At one place, too, they found that
a landslide had completely blocked the path, and it
took four anxious days of hard labor to cut out a new
one for the horses and elephants in the side of the
rocky cliff.

But, through all their trials and dangers, Hannibal
cheered and encouraged the army. When they
reached a height from which the rich plain of the valley of the River Po could be seen in the distance, he
called his men about him, and pointing to it, cried:

"There is Italy! There are friends waiting to welcome you and aid you against the tyrant Rome! You
have now climbed not only the walls of Italy, but of
Rome itself; and after one, or at most two, battles,
all these fertile fields will be yours."

Then the soldiers pushed on with new courage; and
on the fifteenth day after they had entered the Alps,
they came out on the other side of them, in Italy.
But the army was terribly weakened by the hardships

of the way and the fights with the natives. More than half of the men and horses, and many of the elephants, had been lost; and the soldiers who remained were so broken and worn by their sufferings that they looked not like men, but the shadows of men.

Still, the courage of Hannibal did not fail him. He camped his soldiers at the foot of the Alps among friendly tribes of the Gauls, and allowed them to rest and refresh themselves for several days, while the poor lean horses were turned out to pasture. Soon, inspired by his brave spirit, all were ready once more to follow wherever he chose to lead them.

The Romans had not expected that Hannibal would attempt to cross the Alps and carry the war into Italy; or, if any of them did expect it, they had no idea that he would be so soon upon them. When news came that the Carthaginian was already in Italy, they were surprised and dismayed; but still they hurriedly gathered together their forces, and sent them on to meet the enemy.

Any one but Hannibal they might have stopped, but him they could not check. He defeated them in battle after battle, and swept on through their country, with his little army, in a torrent that could not be resisted. The Romans fought desperately, aroused by fear for the city itself; but the armies that faced Hannibal were destroyed in quick succession. In one battle the Romans lost nearly 70,000 men, including eighty senators; and the Carthaginians gathered from the rich men who had fallen on that field enough gold rings to fill a bushel measure. After that, the name of Hannibal became a word of fear to old and young alike; and nearly two hundred years from this time, the memory of that terror still lingered. A Roman poet then wrote of him, calling him "the dread Hannibal," and saying that his march through Italy was like the sweep of the eastern gales that had wrecked so many Roman fleets in the waters of Sicily, or like the rush of flames through a blazing forest of pines.

The Romans had learned how to defeat the Gauls and the Greeks in battle, but they were long in learning how to defeat Hannibal. He was greater than they, and, as long as he remained in Italy, the city of Rome trembled. But the Senate remained strong in the midst of the public terror, and while the people mourned for their dead, the senators only sought men for another army to take the place of the one that had last been destroyed. Their generals, too, though they could not repulse Hannibal in battle, learned to be cautious. They would no longer lead their armies out to fight against him, but hung about watching his camp, in order to capture any of the Carthaginians who might become separated from the main body while gathering food for themselves or for their horses. In this way, they sought to reduce Hannibal by cutting off his supplies, and so make it necessary at last for him to leave Italy of his own accord.

In the end, Rome succeeded, as she always did. "The Romans," said an old writer who described this war, "are never so dangerous as when they seem just about to be conquered." Hannibal found, as Pyrrhus had done before him, that he was fighting a people who could replace a defeated army with another which was just as ready as the first to fight to the death

Most of the peoples of Italy, too, remained faithful to Rome in this time of trial; and Hannibal was disappointed in getting the help from them, against their conqueror, upon which he had counted. So, at last, he was forced to look to Africa and to Spain for new men, and supplies for his army. But when his brother came over the Alps, bringing him help from Spain, he was defeated and slain by the Romans before Hannibal knew that he was in Italy. Besides this, the Senate found men and ships enough to carry the war over into Spain and Africa; and, by and by, the Carthaginians were forced to order Hannibal back from Italy to defend Carthage itself against the attacks of Rome.

So, after fifteen years of victories, which had brought the war no nearer to a close, Hannibal was obliged to leave Italy and return to Africa, for the first time since he had left there, as a boy. When he arrived, he found Carthage much weakened by the war. The general in command of the Roman army was Publius Cornelius Scipio, or "Scipio Africanus," as he soon came to be called, from his deeds in Africa. He was an able general, and had just brought the war in Spain to an end; where, as he reported to the Senate, he "had fought with four generals and four victorious armies, and had not left a single Carthaginian soldier in the peninsula." Now he was to do something greater still, something that no Roman had ever yet done,—that is, to defeat Hannibal in an open battle.

This battle took place near a little town called Zama, which was about two hundred miles inland from Carthage. Scipio had more troops than Hannibal, but

Hannibal had about eighty elephants, and he hoped to win the battle with these. The Romans, however, were now thoroughly used to fighting against elephants; they opened great lanes in their ranks, and let them pass harmlessly through, while the soldiers hurled spears and other weapons at them to drive them along or turn them back. Then the Roman foot-soldiers charged the Carthaginians, shouting their war-cry and clashing their swords against their shields. After a hard fight the soldiers of Hannibal were overcome, and the general alone with a few of his horsemen succeeded in escaping.

SCIPIO AFRICANUS.

Then Hannibal at once advised the Carthaginian Senate to make peace. But the terms of this were much harder than they had been at the close of the first war. Carthage had to give up all of her possessions outside of Africa, and surrender her elephants and all of her warships but ten. She had also to pay an indemnity of about twelve million dollars to Rome, and to agree never to make war on any one without the consent of the Roman Senate. In this way, Carthage ceased to be the head of a great empire, and became merely the ruler of a little strip of territory along the coast of Africa.

After the treaty was signed, Hannibal remained at Carthage, and tried faithfully to help his country in peace as he had helped her in war. But the Romans feared him still and distrusted him; so before many years had passed, he was forced to fly from the city to avoid being put to death by their orders. After that, he wandered about from kingdom to kingdom, on the eastern shores of the Mediterranean; but wherever he went, Roman messengers followed, and would not let him rest in peace. At last, after thirteen years of wandering, he was forced to take his own life to avoid falling into the hands of his unforgiving enemies.

XX

Rome Conquers the World.

THE victory which Rome had won over Hannibal meant something more to the Romans than saving their country from the Carthaginians. It meant the spread of Roman rule from Italy and Sicily over into Africa, Spain, and Greece, and even into Asia. For the Carthaginians were the only people of that day who were strong enough to resist the Romans for any length of time. When they were defeated, at last, there was no other nation in the world that could oppose the power of Rome successfully.

But the growth of Roman territory did not result entirely from the destruction of Carthage. The Romans were now the only people that knew how to rule well, and could put down pirates and robbers, and make the world safe for men to live in. Whenever trouble arose in any country, they would interfere; then it would not be long before the old government would cease, and the Romans would be ruling there as in their own land. Before sixty years had passed from the close of the second war with Carthage, Rome had, in this way, obtained control of almost all the lands that border upon the Mediterranean Sea; and she had gained this great power without any one planning it beforehand, or intending to bring it about.

The Romans took possession of these various coun-

tries in the following order. They received Sicily,
you will remember, after the first war with Carthage.
During the second war, while Hannibal was in Italy,
they conquered Spain; and they kept it for themselves
after this war was over. Then they felt the need of

conquering northern Italy and southern Gaul, so that
their armies could march from Rome to Spain without
being attacked by enemies on the way. This land
also was added to the Roman territory, and almost all
the western part of the Mediterranean world was thus
united under their rule.

It was not long before the Romans reached out into the eastern Mediterranean also. Just north of Greece was a country called Macedonia, whose king had sent soldiers to Hannibal, at the battle of Zama, to aid him against the Romans. To punish him for this, the Romans made war upon him, and defeated him; and, when his son Perseus took up arms after his father's death, they conquered him also. Then the Romans began to rule over Macedonia, and over Greece as well, for the Greeks had long been governed by the Macedonians, and were now no longer able to rule themselves. After this they even went across to Asia Minor and made war on a great king there, who was interfering with affairs in Europe, and moreover, giving shelter to Hannibal, after they had caused him to be driven from Carthage. In this war, the Romans were easily victorious; and then all of Asia that lay along the Mediterranean came under their influence, in addition to their European possessions.

By this time, the Roman name had become a great and dreaded one among all the surrounding nations. Whenever the ruler of a country was threatened by an enemy, and was too weak to meet him alone, his first thought was to call upon the Romans for help. In this way the ruler of Egypt begged the aid of Rome, when a neighboring king made war upon his country. The Senate sent an ambassador to this king, and when they met the Roman drew a circle with his staff on the ground about the king, saying:

"Before you step out of the circle which I have drawn, answer this question, O King. Which will you do, give up your war upon Egypt and have Rome for your friend; or continue it and have Rome for your enemy?"

It did not take the king long to decide that it was best to give up the war. After that the Romans had much influence in Egypt, because they had saved the country from its enemies; and in the course of time, it too was joined to the Roman lands.

In the meantime, Carthage had been slowly recovering from her last war with Rome. Once more, her streets were filled with citizens and her harbors with ships; and the city was growing strong and wealthy as before. But now a stern old Roman named Cato visited Carthage, and, seeing that the city was recovering its prosperity, he feared that it might again become able to fight with Rome on equal terms. When he returned to Italy he bore away with him a bunch of fine figs, plucked in the gardens of Carthage. Upon reaching Rome, he spoke long and earnestly in the Senate of the danger which the Carthaginians might yet be able to bring upon the city, and then he showed to the senators the fresh figs which he had brought back with him.

"The country where these grew is but three days' sail from Rome," he said. "Carthage should be destroyed."

Afterwards this was the constant burden of his talk. He never ended a speech, upon whatever subject, without adding, "And, moreover, I think that Carthage should be destroyed."

At last Cato persuaded the Romans to make war upon Carthage a third time. In spite of the brave defense of the city by the Carthaginians, when even the women and children joined in the fight, the Romans were victorious once more. This time the city was utterly destroyed, and the ground upon which the buildings had stood was ploughed over and sowed with salt, so that it might never more be used by men, or even covered by growing things again. Then Rome began to rule the land about Carthage, and so gained control of most of the northern coast of Africa.

The city of Rome now held sway over more of the world than any nation before that time, and besides ruling this great stretch of country, her citizens made it their own in another way. In whatever region the Romans went, they made their aqueducts, built bridges, and raised public buildings, as they had been doing for so long in Italy itself. Above all, they built good roads to all the lands that came under their rule, so that they might send armies swiftly from one country to another whenever there was need. Along these roads they placed milestones, in order that travelers might know at any time just what their distance was from Rome; and where the towns were far apart, stations were built by the way at which they might rest and hire fresh horses to carry them on their journey to the next stopping-place. So, traveling by land became much easier than it had ever been before, and distant countries seemed to be drawn closer together, just as they have been in our own day by the construction of railroads and the stringing of telegraph wires.

But Rome could not go out over the world and build and rule in all the Mediterranean countries, without this making a great difference in the Romans themselves. Their great men were no longer like Cincinnatus, who left the plough to fight for his country and then went back again when the danger was past. The Roman generals were now very rich men, and they spent all their time in war or in the public business of their country. Moreover, instead of refusing the gifts of kings, as Fabricius had refused the gold of Pyrrhus, it was said that the Roman generals asked for money wherever they went about the world.

The common soldiers, too, were not so good as they had been in the old days. Then each man fought in the army without pay, and supported himself and his family in time of peace by means of his little farm. But now many men began to make a business of fighting, and to serve in the army for a living. As these men did not fight solely for the love of their country, but rather for the money that they got by it, they began to grumble when they were commanded to do things that they did not fancy, and sometimes they would refuse outright to obey their orders.

With such generals and such soldiers, it is not surprising that the Romans were now sometimes shamefully defeated in battle. When they were carrying on the war in Macedonia with King Perseus, the first armies that were sent against him were beaten for just this reason. Then the Romans saw that there must be some change made, and they chose a general of the old-fashioned sort to take the command. His name was Æmilius Paulus, and he was a poor man still, although he could easily have been rich if he had been willing to do as other men were doing. He had been one of the generals in Spain, and also in the north of Italy, and in both places he had shown that he knew how to manage his armies and to gain victories. So the people agreed that he was the man to send against King Perseus, and, rather against his wishes, they elected him consul, and voted to give him command of the army.

Æmilius did not thank the people after they had chosen him consul, as was usually done. He spoke coldly to them instead.

"I suppose, O Romans, that you have chosen me to lead in this war because you think that I can command better than anybody else. I shall expect, therefore, that you will obey my orders, and not give me orders yourselves; for if you propose to command your own commander, you will only make my defeat worse than the former ones."

When Æmilius came to the army in Greece, he saw that the first thing to do was to teach the soldiers to obey orders. He kept them in camp and drilled them for many days; and when they murmured and wanted to be led out to battle, he only replied:

"Soldiers! you should not meddle with what does not concern you. It is your business only to see that you and your arms are ready when the order comes, and that, when your commander gives the word, you use your swords as Romans should."

In this way, Æmilius trained his army; and when the battle was fought, the Romans won a great victory. King Perseus and his children and all his treasures were captured, and his country was brought under the Roman rule. But Æmilius would not so much as go to see the heaps of gold and silver which had been taken from the king's palaces. Instead of making himself and his friends rich from it, he commanded that it should all be sent to Rome and placed in the public treasury; and the amount of it was so great that never after that did Rome have need to raise a war tax from her own people.

The common soldiers, however, were angry at this action of Æmilius, for they wanted to divide the spoil among themselves. Moreover, they disliked him because he ruled them so strictly; so, when the army had returned to Rome, and it was proposed that Æmilius should be allowed a triumph, the soldiers opposed the motion before the people. But an old general who had commanded in many wars arose, and answered them.

"It is now clearer than ever to my mind," he said, "how great a commander our Æmilius is; for I see that he was able to do such great deeds with an army full of baseness and grumbling."

At this, the soldiers were so ashamed that they let the people vote the triumph for Æmilius. When the time for the celebration came, seats were set up in the Forum and in all parts of the city where the show could best be seen. On these the Roman people took their places, dressed in white garments and ready for the great holiday. The temples were all open and filled with flowers and garlands, and the main streets were cleared, and kept open by officers who drove back all who crowded into them. Then came the great procession, which delighted the people for three days.

On the first day, tw hundred and fifty chariots passed, filled with pictures and statues which had been taken from the Greeks. Upon the next day, the rich armor which had been captured was shown; and it made a fine sight, with the light glancing from the polished helmets and shields, and with the swords and spears

TRIUMPHAL PROCESSION.

rattling about among the armor. After these wagons marched three thousand men, each bearing a basin full of silver coin; and following them came others, displaying the silver bowls, goblets, and cups which had been taken.

But the third day furnished the finest sight of all. First, early in the morning, the trumpeters marched along sounding such notes as the Romans used to encourage their soldiers in battle. Then came young men wearing robes with ornamented borders, and leading one hundred and twenty fat oxen, all with their horns gilded, and with ribbons and garlands of flowers tied about their heads. These were for the sacrifices to the gods, which were to be offered at the temples on the Capitol; and with them were boys bearing basins of gold and silver to be used by the priests in the offerings.

After the cattle for the sacrifices walked seventy-seven men, each carrying a basin filled with gold coin; and with them marched those who bore the golden goblets and dishes which King Perseus had used at his table. The chariot of the king came next with his armor in it, and his crown lying on top of that; and the king's little children, two boys and a girl, followed with their attendants and teachers. As they passed along, the servants wept and stretched out their hands, begging the Romans to show mercy to the little princes; and even among those stern conquerors, many hearts were touched at the sight of the unfortunate children.

Then, at a little distance, came King Perseus himself, clothed all in black, and walking quite alone, so that all the people might have a good view of him. After the king and his attendants had gone past, Æmilius appeared, dressed in a robe of purple mixed with gold, and riding in a splendid chariot, holding in his right hand a laurel branch. Following the chariot marched all the army, also bearing laurel branches and singing songs of victory,—just as though they had been the most obedient soldiers in the world. And so the triumph ended.

Many years before, you will remember, the Roman people had crowded the Forum to see Marcus Curtius leap into the chasm and sacrifice himself for the good of his country. What a different sight they had now come to watch—their great army returning home in triumph, burdened with the wealth of a conquered people, and a king and his little children walking into cruel captivity before the chariot of their general! The power of Rome had indeed grown enormously in the meantime, but you can decide for yourself which of the two sights would be likely to have the noblest influence upon the spectators,—the triumph or the sacrifice.

XXI

The Gracchi and Their Mother.

AFTER having watched the splendid triumph of
Æmilius, let us see one of the more common
sights of the city,—a Roman wedding. You will find
it oddly different from the weddings you may have
seen among our own people, but however strange these
old customs seem to be, you must remember that they
were very sacred to the Romans.

The most important part of the wedding ceremony
took place at the house of the bridegroom. First, at
her own home, the bride was dressed in a garment
made all of one piece of cloth, without any seams, and
fastened about the waist with a woolen belt or girdle.
Her hair was parted, not with a comb, but with the
point of a spear, and arranged in six little curls; after
which a yellow net or veil was thrown over her head.
Then in the evening, a procession was formed by the
friends of both families, and the bride was taken from
her father's house to that of her husband. Along the
way minstrels played on their harps, and bridal songs
were sung, while a little boy marched on before,
carrying a blazing torch made from the wood of the
white-thorn tree.

When the procession came to the door of the bridegroom, the bride wrapped the doorposts with sacred
fillets of white wool, and smeared them with oil or fat;

after which she was carefully lifted over the doorsill by her husband. The Romans themselves did not understand the latter custom. Some thought that it was done so that the bride might not stumble upon entering her husband's house for the first time, as that would have been a very bad sign. Others said that it was repeated in memory of the time when the followers of Romulus took wives from the Sabine women by force.

After the procession had entered the house, the bride turned and said to her husband:

"Where thou art, Caius, there will I, Caia, be also."

Next the husband presented her with fire and water, to show that she was now a member of his family, and could sit at his hearth and join in the worship of his household gods. The ceremony was then ended by a feast, with a wedding cake and abundance of nuts.

This is the manner in which Cornelia, the daughter of Scipio Africanus, was married to Tiberius Gracchus. He was a fine soldier and a just and honorable man; and she was then a beautiful girl, who had all the noblest qualities of the great family to which she belonged. For years afterwards they lived happily together, and had many children. Then, according to the story, Tiberius found in their sleeping-room one day a pair of large snakes. The Romans regarded reptiles as sacred, so he went to the priests and asked what he should do with the creatures. They answered that he must kill one and let the other go; and they added, that if he killed the female snake, Cornelia would die, and that if he killed the male, he himself would shortly perish. Tiberius loved his wife deeply, so, when he was told this, he went home and killed the male snake, and let the female escape.

Shortly afterwards Tiberius died, and then his widow, Cornelia, lived only for her children. Even when the king of Egypt sent to her and wished her to become his queen, she would not consent. Only three of her children—two boys and a girl—lived to reach manhood and womanhood; and on these Cornelia centered all of her love and care. She lived with them, and played with them, and taught them their letters; and, as she was a noble, high-minded woman, her children grew to be like her, brave, honorable, and unselfish.

One day, as Cornelia was sitting at home with the children playing near at hand, a lady came to visit her. As they talked the visitor showed her the splendid rings and precious stones which she wore, and at last asked to see her own jewels.

Then Cornelia called her little children, and led them proudly before her guest.

"These are my jewels," she said.

As her boys grew up to be men, Cornelia would sometimes reproach them that she was still known as the relative of the Scipios, and not as the mother of the Gracchi. In this way she made them long to do great deeds, so as to bring her honor; and when the elder of the two boys, Tiberius, came to enter the army, he went at his work with so much earnestness that in a short time he excelled all the other young men in skill at arms. While the Romans were making war on Carthage for the third time, Tiberius Gracchus was the first man to climb up on the wall of the city; and when he was in Spain, fighting with the mountain tribes, he saved the whole army from being destroyed as a result of the faults and mistakes of its commander.

But it is not for what he did as a soldier that Tiberius Gracchus has been remembered. It is rather for what he undertook after he returned to Rome and became a tribune of the people. In spite of all the wealth and power that now came to Rome from her conquered countries, the condition of the common people had become serious, and they needed the aid of a wise tribune more even than in former days. During the terrible war with Hannibal, the small farmers had their property ruined, and fled to the city. After the war was over, the land gradually passed into the hands of the senators and rich men of Rome, and a few great farms took the place of many small ones. The worst of it was that these large farms were not tilled by free laborers, but by slaves,—captives taken in war, for the most part. So the poor freeman not only lost his land, but he lost the chance to work for hire also. The only thing he could do after that was either to enlist in the army and earn his living as a soldier, or else remain idly at Rome and demand that the state should provide for him. The rich candidates for offices were so eager to get the aid of the poorer citizens that they gladly bought their votes by feeding them, and amusing them with games and various spectacles. But, in this way, both the rich and the poor became selfish and greedy, and thought only of what would help themselves, instead of what would be best for the whole people.

Tiberius Gracchus saw these evils, and when he became tribune, he tried to cure them. Much of the land which the rich men held really belonged to the state, though it had been in the hands of private citizens for so many years that the people who held it had begun to forget that they did not really own it. What Gracchus proposed to do was to divide this land among the poor citizens, and build up once more a strong class of small landholders, such as had been the strength of Rome in earlier times.

Of course, the men who already had the land did not favor this plan; so, when Gracchus brought forward his law for the people to vote on it, they got another tribune, named Octavius, to veto it, and that stopped the voting. Then, when Gracchus found that Octavius would not withdraw his veto, he had the people put him out of his office and elect a new tribune in his place. This was against the law, but Gracchus could see no other way of carrying his measure through.

After this, the law which Gracchus had proposed was passed, and he and two other men were appointed to make the distribution of the lands. Before the work was done, however, Gracchus's year of office was over; and he was afraid that, as soon as he should be out of office, the rich citizens would not only find some way to interfere with the law, but that they would also punish him for his treatment of Octavius. At this time no one had ever been allowed to be tribune two years in succession; but Tiberius decided to disobey the laws once more, and have himself elected tribune a second time.

When the senators and rich citizens heard this, they were very angry, and determined to prevent it. Upon the day of the election Gracchus was accused of trying to make himself king and a riot broke out. Then the senators and rich men armed themselves with clubs and bits of benches and stools, and set upon the poorer citizens; and Tiberius Gracchus and three hundred of his followers were slain.

Gracchus had been wrong in putting Octavius out of office, and in trying to get himself elected tribune a second time against the laws. But how much worse was the action of the senators and wealthy citizens! In the old days, when the patricians and the plebeians struggled together, they did so peaceably and with respect for the laws. Now, in these new strifes between the party of the poor and the party of the rich, force was used for the first time, and men were killed in a political struggle at Rome. And for this the senators and rich men were chiefly to blame.

The younger of the Gracchi, Caius, was not at Rome when Tiberius was killed. He was still a very young man, just beginning his training as a soldier, and for ten years longer he went on serving with the armies of Rome. Then, although the Senate tried unlawfully to keep him from returning to the city, he came back, and he too was elected tribune.

Caius was much more rash than his brother had been. In spite of all that his mother Cornelia could do to prevent it, he resolved to carry out the plans of his brother Tiberius, and even to go further. He wanted to overturn the government by the Senate and the nobles, and put in its place a government by the people, with himself at their head. He got the support of the people for this by passing a law that they should always have grain sold to them at a low price. Then he gained the support of many of the wealthy citizens, by passing laws which took rights and privileges from the senators, and gave them to the rich men who were not senators.

So Caius Gracchus obtained more power than his brother had possessed; and a law having now been passed which permitted one to be re-elected as tribune, he was allowed to serve a second time. After this, he was able to pass many laws to help the poorer citizens. But when he wished to do still more, and aid the Italians who were not citizens of Rome, his followers selfishly deserted him. They were afraid that they would have to share their cheap grain and their free games with the Italians, so this law was not passed; and, at the next election, Caius Gracchus was not made tribune again.

Then Gracchus tried to live quietly, as a private citizen, at Rome. But now that he was no longer tribune, the nobles soon found ways in which to quarrel with him; and when a riot again broke out, Caius and many of his friends were put to death by the senators, as Tiberius Gracchus had been before them.

You would think that, after the death of her second son, poor Cornelia would have been heart-broken and would almost have hated her country, for the ingratitude with which its people had treated her children. But the Romans believed that you ought not to show sorrow at anything that happened to you, no matter how dreadful it might be. So Cornelia put on a brave face, hiding the suffering that was in her heart; and when she spoke of the deeds and deaths of her sons, it was without a sigh or a tear, as if she were talking about some of the ancient heroes who had died ages before. Every one admired her for her courage and virtue; and in time the Roman people repented of their conduct towards her sons, and began to look upon them as the truest friends they had ever had. When Cornelia died, a statue was set up in her honor, and underneath it were carved these words, as her best title to remembrance:

"Cornelia, the mother of the Gracchi."

XXII

The Wars of Caius Marius.

CAIUS MARIUS was a poor country lad who entered the army as a common soldier, and, without the help of money or of a powerful family rose to the highest position. It is said that when he was a boy, he one day caught in his cloak an eagle's nest, with seven young ones in it, as it was falling from a high tree. From this the wise men foretold that he should be seven times consul; and Marius never rested until this saying had come true.

He gained his first knowledge of war in Spain under Scipio Æmilianus. This Scipio was the son of Æmilius Paulus, the conqueror of Macedonia, and an adopted son in the family of the great Scipio Africanus. As he was also an able and honorable man, he was thus a very good master under whom to learn the art of war; and Caius Marius profited well by the lessons which he learned in his camp. When the commander was asked one day where the Romans would ever find as good a general as himself when he was gone, he turned and touched the shoulder of young Marius, who stood near.

"Here, perhaps," he replied.

This encouraged Marius, and he struggled on for many years, gradually rising in the army and in the state from one position to another. At last he even succeeded in having himself elected consul, and so received the command of an army himself.

His opportunity came in this way. A king named Jugurtha arose in a little kingdom near Carthage, gaining his power in a most unjust manner, and then using it in a way that was even worse. At last the Roman Senate was forced to declare war upon him. It proved that he was not to be easily conquered, and the Roman generals who were sent against him did not seem to be able to bring the trouble to an end. Finally Marius, who was with one of the generals as second in command, became very impatient over this delay in crushing Jugurtha, and resolved to go to Rome and try to get the command for himself.

Marius was very well liked by the common soldiers because he had been one of themselves, and still ate the same coarse food and slept upon the same beds that they did, often helping them with his own hands in digging ditches and throwing up earthworks. But the general of the army scorned him because of his low birth; and when Marius applied to him for permission to go to Rome to become a candidate for consul, he laughed at him.

"It will be time enough for you to become candidate for consul when my young son does," he said.

Marius left the army deeply angered, and when he came to Rome he showed that he had more influence than had been suspected. He told the people how slowly the war was going on and how much better he could manage it himself. As he belonged to their own class, the common people believed him and elected him consul, giving him by a special vote the command of the army against Jugurtha.

When Marius returned to Africa, he found that it was more difficult to bring the war to an end than he had expected. But at last Jugurtha was betrayed to him by one of his own household, and then Marius ended the war and brought the king captive to Rome. No sooner was this war over than another one broke out which threatened the Romans with such a terrible danger that they elected Marius consul a second time to meet this new enemy; and then a third and a fourth time. At last he had been consul for five terms before the danger was past, and it seemed as though the old prophecy concerning him might yet be fulfilled.

This new war was with a people who came from the region north of the Alps and overran Gaul, threatening to pass into Italy. Although they were called by several names, they were probably Germans, and belonged to the same family of nations from which the Germans of to-day, the English, and most of the Americans are descended. Large and strong of body, and as hardy as they were strong, they terrified the Romans more even than the Gauls had done two hundred and eighty years before. Like the Gauls, they came in great numbers, carrying their wives and children and all their possessions with them in rude, covered wagons, and went wandering about looking for a new home in which to settle.

The Romans first met these newcomers in that part of Gaul which had come under Roman rule. There, four great armies of the Romans were destroyed one after the other. Then it was that Marius was elected consul a second time, and sent into Gaul to keep these Germans from crossing the Alps and reaching Italy. Fortunately for the Romans, the barbarians turned aside into Spain after their last great victory, and remained in that country for two or three years. Thus Marius had time to get together a new army, and to drill his men thoroughly. When the barbarians came back from Spain, they separated,—one band of them starting north around the Alps in order to enter Italy from the east, while the others remained in Gaul, and tried to reach the peninsula from the western side.

Even after so large a part of the Germans had left Gaul, Marius did not dare to lead his men out of camp against those that remained. For six days he let them march continuously past his camp; and as they went by they shouted taunts to the Romans and asked whether they had any messages to send to their wives. But when the last of this band, too, had disappeared, Marius led his army out, and followed them. He came up with them just before they reached the Alps, and by this time he had his soldiers so well trained that he decided to risk a battle. The result was a great victory for the Romans; for the barbarians were entirely destroyed, and their kings were made captives.

Then Marius hurried on into Italy and marched to the aid of the other consul, who had been sent to meet the band that was seeking to enter the peninsula from the east. This consul was not so good a general as Marius, and the barbarians succeeded in getting into the country on that side. When Marius arrived, they sent to him and demanded lands in Italy on which they and their brethren, whom they had left in Gaul, might settle.

In reply, Marius showed them the captives who had been brought with him and the Germans were filled with grief and anger, for they knew that their brethren had been destroyed. Though they might well have feared the same fate for themselves, the chiefs of their army challenged Marius to fix the time and place for a battle. He chose the third day after that and a broad plain near by for the place. When the battle came, the Germans fought with great bravery, and their women, standing in the wagons, encouraged their husbands and brothers with fierce cries; but at last the Romans were victorious and this band of the barbarians was also destroyed.

After this Marius returned to Rome, where he was received with great honor and rejoicing. Men called him the third founder of the city; for they said, that just as Camillus had saved Rome from the Gauls, so Marius had saved it from these new invaders. As a reward for his victories he was soon after elected consul for the sixth time.

If Marius had been a statesman as well as a soldier, he might now have used his power to remedy the evils which the Gracchi had tried to cure, and so have saved the state. But though Marius could win battles, he could not govern in time of peace. Long after this men said of him that "he never cared to be a good man, so he was a great one"; and perhaps that is the reason he failed as a ruler. He hesitated to take either the side of the common people, or that of the nobles, for he wished only to do the thing that would benefit himself. In this way Marius lost the influence which he had gained by his victories; and for twelve

years the conqueror of the Germans was despised and neglected by everyone.

At last civil war began between the party of the common people and the party of the nobles. The latter had a famous soldier named Sulla as commander of their army; and the leaders of the common people chose Marius, although he was then nearly seventy years old, to be their general. Marius had long been jealous of Sulla, and besides he was eager to gain the seventh consulship that had been promised him, so he accepted the command. But at first the nobles got the better of the party of Marius; and when Sulla marched on Rome, the city was taken by his army. This was the first capture of Rome by a body of its own citizens, but it was not to be the last.

SULLA.

When Rome was taken by Sulla, Marius escaped with much difficulty, and for many days wandered about Italy with only a few companions. At one time they barely escaped a party of horsemen on the shore by swimming out to some ships which were sailing by. At another they lay hid in a marsh with the mud and water up to their necks. Once Marius was taken prisoner, and the officers of the town where he was held sent a Gaulish slave to kill him in his dungeon; but Marius's eyes gleamed so fiercely in the darkness as he called out in a loud voice, "Fellow, darest thou kill Caius Marius?" that the slave dropped his sword and fled. Then the officers of the town faltered in their purpose and at last allowed Marius to go free. He escaped to the neighborhood of Carthage, but even there he was not safe, for the Roman governor of that district sent a message warning him to leave. When the command was given to him, Marius replied, "Go, tell the governor that you have seen Caius Marius sitting in exile among the ruins of Carthage."

At last Sulla was obliged to leave Italy and go to Asia Minor to make war on a powerful king in that region. Then the friends of Marius got control of Rome once more; and Marius could safely return. When he came back his heart was filled with rage against his enemies, and he caused thousands of them to be put to death without trial or hearing. Even his friends came to fear this gloomy and revengeful man. He gained his seventh consulship at this time, but he did not live long to enjoy it. His many years of war and bloodshed had left him a strange old man, full of bitterness and unrest. Finally he died, on the seventeenth day of his seventh consulship; and the whole people breathed freer when he was gone.

Soon afterwards Sulla returned from the east, and when he had regained his power he took a terrible revenge on all the friends of Marius. Many persons were put to death simply because some one of Sulla's friends desired their property. The Italian cities which had rebelled against Rome in this time of trouble were punished with great severity, and so terribly was Italy wasted that it seemed as if Hannibal had come again.

XXIII

Cicero, the Orator.

AT the close of the war with Jugurtha a child was born in Marius's old home near Rome, who was to become as famous as Marius himself, but in a better and nobler way. Marcus Tullius Cicero was to be a great orator and writer, and rule the state by his eloquence as others governed it by force of arms. This would have been impossible in the earlier city, when the consuls had to be generals first of all, and the education of the citizens consisted mainly in training for battle. In these later times, however, the people studied something besides the use of arms and the laws of their city; and Cicero, who was a scholar instead of a soldier, was chosen to govern them as consul.

It is very interesting to compare the education of a Roman like Cicero with that which is given almost every boy and girl of our own day. Cicero's parents lived outside of Rome, and he was sent from his country home to his uncle in the city at the age of six, in order to enter school there. Before this his training had been mostly in charge of his mother, except when he stood at the family altar watching his father's sacrifices to the gods; or, perhaps, when he learned to speak Greek even so early, by listening to the talk of some slave brought from that country as a captive.

From his infancy he had been told the stories of the Roman heroes, and of his own ancestors, and taught by means of them to be modest, brave, and obedient. But this was only for family instruction; the school at Rome, to which he was sent so young, dealt with the usual general subjects.

In the city the schools then began at sunrise, and

ROMAN BOOKS AND WRITING MATERIALS.

In two of the pictures purses and heaps of coins are also shown.

the children had to be up and ready to start before daybreak. They carried lanterns to light their way, and slaves went with them to and fro so that no harm might befall them. In the schoolroom, the master sat on a raised platform at one end of the room, with the children on stools and benches in front of him. Around the walls there were lyres, or harps, to be used in the music lessons, and also pictures of the gods or of scenes from the history of Rome. On one of the walls a board was hung on which were written the names of all absent or truant pupils. Above the master's bench there was a great stick, and the lazy boys had good reason to fear it when they did not know their lessons.

In this lowest school, the children learned to read and to write. Instead of slates or sheets of paper, they had wooden tablets covered with wax; and on these they wrote with a sharp-pointed instrument called a stylus. The other end of the stylus was blunt, so that when a pupil made a mistake in his writing, he could smooth it out in the soft wax with this end, and then try again. Here the children also learned arithmetic. Perhaps the arithmetic which you have to study is difficult for you; but think how much harder it must have been for the Roman boys. They did not have the plain and easy figures which you use, but only what we still call the "Roman numerals." If you want to see how much more difficult it is to use these, try to find the answer to

XXIV times LXXXVII,

and then see how much easier it is when it is written

24 times 87.

Because their arithmetic was so hard, each Roman boy carried with him to school a counting-frame to help him. This was a wooden contrivance divided into lines and columns, and he worked his problems with it by putting little pebbles in the different columns to represent the different denominations.

After Cicero had gone through this school, he entered what was called a grammar school. There he studied Greek grammar, and read some of the famous books of that day, both Greek and Latin. Of course these were not printed books, as printing was not invented for fifteen hundred years after this. Those which he studied were all written with a pen, on smooth white skins called parchment, or on paper made from the papyrus plant which grows in Egypt. Instead of being bound as our books are, the pages of these were all pasted into one long strip, and then rolled tightly around a stick.

In such a school young Cicero studied until he was fifteen years old. Up to that time he had worn the "boyish toga," with its narrow purple border, and carried a "bulla" or charm about his neck to ward off the evil eye. After he passed that age, he discarded the boyish toga and the bulla, and put on for the first time a toga all of white, such as the men wore. This was made a day of festival for the family, and the young man went with his father and his friends into the Forum, where his name was written in the list of Roman citizens, and then to the temples on the Capitol to offer sacrifices to the gods. After this he might be called upon to serve in war, and he had the right to vote and to do everything that the grown men were allowed to do.

All Roman boys of good families followed this course of training up to the time when they put on the manly toga. After that, if they intended to prepare themselves for war, they entered the camp of some general and attached themselves to him; but if they intended to train themselves for the law, and become speakers, they attended the law courts in the Forum. Cicero's father wished him to be fitted for the law, so he put the lad in charge of one of the great judges and lawyers of that time. In his company and under his direction, Cicero attended the law courts day after day, and listened to the best speakers, taking notes on all that he saw and heard. Thus, in the course of time, he learned the laws of his country and the ways in which the courts did business; and by constant attention and practice, he also came to be an excellent speaker.

After a number of years spent in this way, Cicero at last had a chance to show the Roman people what good use he had made of his time in the law courts. During the terrible civil war between Marius and Sulla, a young Roman was charged most unjustly with the murder of his father; but all the lawyers of Rome were afraid to defend him, for it was known that whoever did so might anger Sulla, and so bring a sentence of death upon himself. Cicero, however, was willing to risk the danger. He defended the young man before the court, and the cause was so good, and Cicero spoke so well and fearlessly in his behalf, that he was at once released. This gave Cicero some fame at Rome, but he did not dare to remain there afterwards for fear of the wrath of Sulla. So he went to Greece, where he passed his time in studying under Greek masters, and learning how to speak and write still better.

At last news came that Sulla was dead, and Cicero returned to Rome. Then he entered politics, and proved to be such a good speaker, and so honest, and so learned in the laws, that he was elected to one office after another at the very lowest age that he could hold them. Moreover, he received these honors in spite of the fact that the nobles looked upon him with scorn as a man of lower birth, since no member of his family had ever yet been chosen consul.

Though he now held public offices, Cicero did not cease to come before the law courts whenever there was need. At one time a man named Verres was charged with misgoverning the province of Sicily and unlawfully taking large sums of money from them while he was ruling the island. This had come to be a very common thing. Indeed, people would often say that a Roman governor had to make three fortunes out of his province during the time that he was in office: one to pay off the debts he had made to get the office, another to bribe the judges at Rome in case they should try to punish him for his dishonesty, and a third to live on after he returned to Rome. So, although Verres was much worse than governors usually were, few people expected to see him punished. Cicero took charge of this case, and he managed it so skilfully that in spite of all Verres could do he was forced to leave Rome and go into exile. This won for Cicero the praise of all honest citizens, but it is believed that it did not make the Roman governors themselves very much better.

When Cicero had held all of the offices below that of consul, it happened that a plot was made at Rome which nearly overturned the government; and in this time of danger, Cicero was elected consul. The common people and the nobles had once more begun their quarrels, which had been checked during the period of Sulla's stern rule. A ruined noble, named Catiline, now put himself forward as the leader of the common people, and with their support he tried to gain the consulship. But all good men distrusted him, because of the crimes which were charged against him, and because it was known that he was deeply in

CICERO.

debt and ready to do anything to get money. So the moderate men among both the common people and the nobles united in supporting Cicero for consul against Catiline, and Cicero was elected.

Thereupon Catiline determined to secure by force what he could not get by the vote of the people. He drew together a number of ruined nobles like himself, and planned with them to murder the consuls and seize the city, in order to burn and rob as they chose.

Cicero was informed of these plans; but he did not dare to arrest Catiline, for he had powerful friends and the consuls did not yet have clear proof of the plot. He decided to rouse and startle Catiline so that he would show his plans openly, and all the people might be convinced of them. Accordingly, Cicero arose in the Senate, while Catiline was there, and made a powerful speech against him.

"How long, O Catiline," he cried, "will you abuse our patience? When will this boldness of yours come to an end? Do not the guards which are placed each night on the Palatine hill alarm you? Do not the watchmen posted throughout the city, does not the alarm of the people and the union of all good men, do not the looks and expressions of the senators here, have any effect upon you? Do you not feel that your plans are known? What did you do last night or the night before that you think is still unknown to us?"

Then Cicero went on to tell all the plans of Catiline, and showed him that so much was known of them that he left the Senate in fright and rage, and rode hastily away from the city to join some soldiers that he had stationed near by. Everyone was convinced by this that what Cicero had claimed was true, and an army was sent against the plotter and his troops. They were easily overcome and Catiline was slain, while his followers in the city were arrested and put to death.

For Cicero's wise government of Rome, at this time, men of both parties honored him, and he was publicly called "the father of his country." But it was not long before the influence which he had gained by his good services was greatly weakened.

Rome had grown, as you have seen, from a little city-state, to be a great empire; but the form of the government was still the same that it had been in the old days. This was not as it should have been, for a great empire could not be ruled like a single city. It was not only unjust, but it was unwise to let a few thousand greedy, selfish men choose the officers and make the laws that were to rule all the millions of people that were governed by Rome. But there seemed to be no way to remedy the trouble, for nobody had then thought of what we call "representative government,"—that is, one in which the people of each city or district elect men to represent them at the capital of the country, and make laws for the whole land. The Romans knew only two ways of governing a great empire: one was to let the people of the chief city rule over all the rest, as Rome was doing; the other was to give up free government altogether, and allow a king to rule the whole according to his will.

Many people thought that the government by the Senate and people of Rome could still continue. Cicero was one of these, and he tried to build up a party in support of this idea; but it was an impossible task. The senators were selfish and shortsighted; the rich men were only anxious for more wealth; and the common people were ready to support any one who would give them bread to eat, and amuse them with races and wild-beast fights. Besides this, there were now several powerful men in Rome who realized that a change in the government must soon come, and each of whom was trying to make himself master of the city.

So Cicero failed in his attempt. First he was exiled from Rome, on a charge of unlawfully punishing some of the followers of Catiline. Then, after he had been allowed to return to Rome, civil war broke out

CIRCUS MAXIMUS.

between the different persons who were trying to get the chief power; and the wars continued until at last the Republic came to an end, and Julius Cæsar, the ablest man among the Romans, gathered up all the offices of the government in his own hands, and made himself sole ruler of the empire.

In this time of terrible civil war, Cicero could have no place, for he was a peaceful man who tried to rule men by persuading them, instead of commanding them by force. When the old government had been finally overthrown, he no longer took an interest in politics. After that, he spent his time in study; and the books which he wrote then may still be read by those who understand the Latin language,—indeed, they have done more to make the name of Cicero famous than anything else that he ever accomplished.

But before many years had passed in this way, Cæsar was slain by some of his enemies, and new struggles began for the mastery of the Roman world. Cicero now thought that perhaps the government by the Senate and people might be renewed, and he spoke and wrote in order to bring this about; but his efforts were all in vain. The attempt to restore the old government failed, and Cicero lost his own life by it. His writings had annoyed and offended some of the great men of Rome, and at last they ordered that he should be put to death.

Long after this, one of the men who had given the command for Cicero's death found his nephew reading a book which the boy vainly tried to hide under his gown. He took possession of it, and found that it was one of Cicero's works. For a long time he stood reading, absorbed in the noble thought and language; then, as he returned the book, he said, "My child, this was a learned man, and one who loved his country well."

XXIV

Julius Cæsar, the Conqueror of Gaul.

CAIUS JULIUS CÆSAR belonged to a noble family, but he was a nephew of Marius by marriage, and it was this perhaps that caused him first to act with the party of the people. He was little more than a boy when Sulla and Marius were carrying on their terrible struggles for the mastery, and he had taken no part in these troubles. But when Sulla had overcome the common people, and was putting to death all persons whom he regarded as the enemies of his own party, he wished to include young Cæsar in the number. Some of the general's firmest friends, however, and even the Vestal Virgins, went to him and begged that Cæsar's life might be spared, because of his youth and his noble birth. For a long time they pleaded in vain, but at last Sulla gave way.

"Let him live, then, as you wish," he said; "but I would have you know that there is many a Marius in this young man, for whose safety you are so anxious. You will find, some day, that he will be the ruin of the party of the nobles to which you and I all belong."

After this narrow escape Cæsar did not dare to stay longer at Rome. He went to the lands about the eastern end of the Mediterranean Sea, and joined the camp of a general who was carrying on one of the conflicts which the Romans were now constantly waging in that region. Here Cæsar got his first training in war; and one day he showed such bravery in saving the life of a fellow soldier, that the commander presented him with a crown of oak leaves. This, as you will remember from the story of Coriolanus, was a mark of high honor among the Romans.

After Sulla was dead, Cæsar returned to Rome; but not to remain there long. He decided that he wished to be an orator as well as a soldier, so he went to Greece, as Cicero had done, to study the art of writing and speaking. While he was on his way there he had an adventure which shows very well the character of the man even in his youth. The ship that he was on was captured by pirates, and Cæsar was told by them that he must pay a large sum of money before they would let him go. He at once sent his servants to raise this sum, but in the meantime he had to stay with the pirates on their island home.

These were desperate men, who considered the crime of murder a trifling act; but Cæsar seemed to have no fear of them, and even showed his contempt for them quite freely. When he wished to sleep, he would order them to be silent while he did so; and in other moods he would join in their rough play and exercise. To help pass away the time till his servants should return he wrote poems and speeches, and recited them to these ignorant men. When they did not seem pleased with his efforts, he frankly called them "dunces" and "barbarians." They accepted all this from Cæsar with great good-humor, for they liked his fearless spirit; and when he threatened to punish them, as soon as he was free, for their piracy and crimes, they only laughed at him and thought it a great joke.

After his money had come, however, and he was at liberty, the first thing that Cæsar did was to carry out this threat. He gathered together some ships and men, and returned to the island where the pirates stayed. Here he found their vessels still at anchor, and in the battle which followed, he defeated them and captured most of the men, recovering also the money which he had paid them as a ransom.

At Rome, after this, Cæsar led the kind of life that was usual among all the wealthy young men of the time. He joined in the gayety of the city, and seemed to think of nothing but that. He was very careful in his dress, and was one of the leaders of the fashion at Rome. This seemed foolish to the grave Cicero, and he once spoke doubtfully of Cæsar, wondering if there could really be any earnest purpose in a man who gave so much thought to the arrangement of his hair.

Beneath this lightness of behavior, however, lay great powers of mind and character. Cæsar had already determined to accomplish something great, and he never lost sight of this purpose. At the very time that Cicero thought him so foolish and careless, he was preparing himself to win the favor of the people and become their leader. When he began to speak in public, he had taken so much pains to train himself well, that he pleased his hearers from the first; and after his return from Greece, he was looked upon as one of the best orators of Rome. He was friendly and pleasant to every one, and gave money freely to all who begged his help. Of course he became very popular, and soon he was elected to several offices, one after the other.

While Cæsar held one of these offices, it was his duty to oversee the public games. The Romans, as you know, had now become very fond of such shows, and they were given a number of times each year in various forms. Some of them were like the Greek games, and were contests in running, wrestling, leaping, and hurling the spear. Others were sham battles, in which little armies of horsemen, infantry, and elephants took part. But those that the Romans liked best were three,—the chariot races, the fights with wild beasts, and the contests of gladiators.

The chariot races were held in a race course called the Great Circus, which lay between the Palatine hill and the one which stood south of it. Each chariot was usually drawn by four horses, and four chariots took part in each race. The drivers of the chariots wore different colored gowns,—white, red, blue, and green; and the people took such interest in these races, that they divided into parties over them. In this way there came to be a party of the Greens, who always favored the driver who wore that color, and a party of the Blues, and so on; while sometimes the people became so excited by the races that they actually came to blows about them.

The custom of chariot races was very old,—indeed, it was said that Romulus first began them; but the wild-beast fights were not introduced until after the second war with Carthage. Then the Romans began to turn elephants, lions, leopards, and other beasts, into the "arena" of the Circus (as the central part of it was called), and set men to hunt them for the amusement of the spectators. It is said that four hundred lions were once fought and killed there at the same time to make sport for the people.

But the shows which delighted the Romans most were the fights of the gladiators. These were men who were trained for fighting to amuse the people; and they were usually captives who had been taken in war, or slaves who had been sold to the trainers of gladiators as a punishment. Most often they fought together in single pairs. Sometimes they were both armed in the same way, with helmet, shield, and sword. Sometimes, however, one only would be

CHARIOT RACE.

armed thus, and the other would have nothing but a three-pointed spear with which to thrust at his enemy, and a net to throw over his head and entangle him. When one of the gladiators became wounded, the fight stopped until the will of the people had been made known. If they held their thumbs up, he was spared; but if they turned them downwards, they

wished to see no mercy shown, and the conquered one was put to death.

The government was supposed to furnish the money to provide for these shows, but it had become the custom for the overseers of the games to add to them at their own expense.

GLADIATOR FIGHT.

When Cæsar was made overseer he tried to give finer spectacles than had ever been seen before, regardless of the cost. Everybody said that there had never been more or better gladiator fights or greater animal hunts than those he furnished. The statues and pictures, too, which he provided to decorate the Forum and the temples on the Capitol during the time of the games, were so numerous that places had to be found elsewhere for many of them.

Cæsar spent such large sums of his own money on these shows that he came out of the office very heavily in debt; but he had succeeded in his purpose. He had made the people think him generous and public-spirited; so when he became a candidate for the consulship some time after this, they gladly supported him. The nobles, however, did not like Cæsar so well, and they opposed his election, for they were already beginning to fear his power over the people. But at this time there was a man at Rome who could aid him greatly with his election, if he would, and he needed Cæsar's help as much as Cæsar needed his.

This man was named Pompey, and he was called "the Great" because of his deeds in war. At one time he had put down a dangerous revolt in Spain. After that he had helped to stamp out a rebellion of gladiators, who had fled in large numbers to Mount Vesuvius in Italy, and formed a strong camp there. Then, some time after Cæsar's adventure with the pirates, Pompey had been given a great fleet and had been commissioned to make war upon them. With this fleet he had started from the Straits of Gibraltar, and searched every nook and corner of the Mediterranean Sea, sweeping all the pirates before him till he reached the coast of Asia. There he defeated them in one great battle, and so cleared the seas of robbers for many years thereafter. Following this, Pompey had been given the command in a war with a king on the southern shore of the Black Sea; and there also he had been successful. At last he had come back to Rome with much honor, and was given a great triumph by the people; but the nobles looked upon him with suspicion, and refused to reward his soldiers, or to approve the arrangements which he had made for the conquered country in the East.

This vexed Pompey exceedingly; so he joined with Cæsar, and they agreed to help each other in gaining what they both wanted. In this way Pompey obtained lands for his soldiers and had his acts in the East approved; and Cæsar received his election as consul. After his year as consul was up, and it was time for him to go as governor to one of the provinces, as was the custom, Cæsar was appointed governor of Gaul for five years. Before that time was passed he was given another term of five years by a new agreement between the two men, while Pompey was appointed to govern Spain for an equal time.

The senators were not sorry to see Cæsar go to Gaul, for they hoped that during his long absence from the city, the fickle people of Rome might forget him, and so leave him without influence when he returned. Or, if this should not happen, they hoped at least that something might occur in the meantime to make his influence less dangerous to the party of the nobles.

At this time there were two districts which the Romans called by the name of Gaul, and Cæsar was given command over both of these. One was on the Italian side of the Alps, and included the lands in the valley of the River Po, on which those Gauls had lived who welcomed Hannibal when he came into Italy. This was called "Cis-Alpine Gaul," or "Gaul on this side of the Alps." The other lay beyond the Alps, in what is now southern France, and this was called "Trans-Alpine Gaul."

Cis-Alpine Gaul had been conquered for some time,

but in Trans-Alpine Gaul the power of the Romans did not extend beyond a little strip of land in the southern part, where the country touches the Mediterranean Sea. Moreover, the affairs of Gaul beyond the Alps had been neglected by the Romans during the late struggles in the city itself, and when Cæsar reached his provinces he found that troubles were beginning there which needed his immediate attention. He was told that a large body of people who lived in the valleys of the Alps, had determined to leave their homes among the mountains, and seek new ones in the western part of Gaul. They had burned their towns and villages, so that their people could have no wish to return to their old homes, and they were now ready to start on their journey through the Roman province, carrying their families and their goods with them.

The march of so large a body of the Swiss through Trans-Alpine Gaul might mean the beginning of much trouble for the Romans; so Cæsar determined that they must be stopped before they had gone any farther from their homes. He crossed the Alps in haste, therefore, and sent word to the Swiss forbidding them to march through his province. Then, when they tried in spite of this to force their way out of the mountains, he defeated them in a terrible battle; and sent them back to their own country, to rebuild their burned homes and settle upon their own lands once more.

This great victory gave Cæsar's soldiers confidence in their new commander; and it also caused many of the neighboring tribes of Gaul to submit to him, and become friends to the Roman people. Soon afterwards the chiefs of one of these tribes appealed to Cæsar for aid in a trouble of their own, begging him to help them against a tribe of Germans, who had lately crossed the Rhine, and come into their lands. These Germans had already conquered a part of the country, and were inviting other German tribes to cross the river and join them in overrunning the whole of Gaul. This would have been more dangerous even than to have had the Swiss pass through the country in search of new homes; so Cæsar determined to give the help that was asked of him, and send the Germans also back to their own lands.

But while Cæsar was preparing to march against the Germans, his army began to give him trouble. The Gauls and the Roman traders, who passed through the camp, told marvelous tales of the great size of the Germans, of the fierceness of their appearance, and of their skill with their weapons. When Cæsar's soldiers heard these stories, and when it was whispered among them that they were about to march against the Germans, they began to fear this people as much as Marius's soldiers had done before them. Some of the young officers, who had had little experience in war, even began to make excuses for being allowed to return to Rome. Others, who were ashamed to leave the army in this way, made their wills, and went about the camp with tears streaming down their faces. These claimed that it was not the enemy they feared; but that they dreaded the narrowness of the roads, and the vastness of the forests through which they would have to pass, and they were afraid, too, that there would not be food enough for the army on its march.

When Cæsar heard these things, he called a meeting of his soldiers and rebuked them.

"Is it your business," he asked, "to inquire in what direction we are to march, and what are the plans of your general? Is it your duty to think of the feeding of the army, and the condition of the roads? That is my affair, and not yours; and you should not distrust me so much as to think that I will not attend to it. I suspect, indeed, that it is the enemy that you dread, and not the dangers of the march. But even though you know that you are to fight against the Germans, what is it that you fear in them? They have already been defeated by Marius within the memory of our fathers. The Swiss, whom you have so lately sent back to their homes, have defeated them in their own country. Shall we not be able to do what they have succeeded in doing? I had intended to put off this march of ours to a more distant day; but now I have determined to break up our camp during this very night, so that I may find out as soon as possible whether my soldiers will answer to the call of duty, or give way to fear. If no others will follow me, I shall still go forward with the tenth legion alone; for I know that the men of that company, at least, are too brave ever to desert their commander."

The fears of the soldiers vanished before the scorn and determination of their general. The tenth legion sent messengers to him to thank him for his confidence in them; and the soldiers of the other legions made excuses for themselves, and begged him to believe that they would follow him wherever he might wish to go. Cæsar accepted their excuses; but that night, as he had said he would, he began the march. When the army came up with the Germans, and a battle was fought, Cæsar easily defeated the enemy, driving them back across the Rhine into their own country.

These two wars were the beginning of Cæsar's command in Gaul. In a few months, he had succeeded in saving the country from being overrun by the Swiss and by the Germans; and perhaps he had even kept the barbarians from entering Italy again as in the time of Marius. He remained governor of Gaul for nine years, and during that time he conquered all the country from the Rhine west to the Atlantic Ocean, and from the Roman province in the south to the English Channel on the north. And several times he even passed these limits. Twice when he wished to overawe the restless tribes of Germany, he quickly built a bridge over the broad Rhine, and led his army across to frighten the neighboring tribes into submission. Twice, also, he gathered ships and went over into the neighboring island of Great Britain, to make war upon the tribes that lived there, and punish them for having interfered in the affairs of Gaul.

Cæsar was the first Roman general to lead an army into either Germany or Britain; and although he made no serious attempt to subdue these countries himself, he prepared the way for the conquest of Britain, at least, in the time that was to come. In Gaul, however, he completely conquered the country. When he left that land its people had already settled down quietly under the Roman rule, and they were beginning to learn the Roman customs and the Roman language. So entirely did they accept these that they became almost like the Romans themselves, and even to-day the language of the country—French—remains a form of the old Latin tongue, which the Roman conquerors spoke nearly two thousand years ago.

One of the things that helped Cæsar most in this great work of conquest was his power over the common soldiers. During all the years that they fought under him in Gaul, they never once repeated the threat of disobedience, which they had made when he first proposed to lead them against the Germans. From that time on they were entirely devoted to him, for they had confidence in him. He was willing to share every danger and hardship with his men, and when he spoke to them he called them "Fellow soldiers," to show that he was one of them. In the marches with his army, he used to go at the head of his troops, sometimes on horseback, but oftener on foot, with his head bare in all kinds of weather. At the beginning of a battle, he often sent his horse away, so that he might lead his men on foot. If they began to give way during the fight he would go among them and stop those who were flying, turning them towards the enemy again; and so by his own courage and determination he would compel them to be victorious.

Cæsar was both mild and strict in his control of his men. After they had won a victory he would allow them to rest and make merry; but before a battle had been fought, he demanded unceasing watchfulness and entire obedience. He would give no notice of battle till the last moment, in order that the soldiers might always hold themselves in readiness for it; and, for the same reason, he would often lead his men out of their camp, when there was no need of it, even in rainy weather and on holidays. Sometimes, either by day or night, he would suddenly give them orders to follow without losing sight of him; and then lead them on long marches in order to test their strength, and to prepare them for doing the same thing whenever there might be real necessity for it. In this way, long before Cæsar's nine years in Gaul were over, he had an army of veterans, every man of whom was willing to follow him into any danger.

While Cæsar was still in Gaul, he wrote an account of his struggles with the barbarians, and sent it to Rome, so that the people might know of the successes of his army. Many of the Roman books have been lost, but Cæsar's own account of his wars in Gaul is so well written and so interesting that it was carefully saved, and if you should ever study Latin, this will be almost the first book that you will read.

XXV

Cæsar and the Beginning of the Empire.

DURING the years of Cæsar's life in Gaul, the mis
government of Rome had been growing steadily
worse. The elections for consuls could not be held
without disorder, and the candidates for office went
about with bands of armed men for their protection.
Sometimes these bands actually fought at the voting
places; and once the election of consuls was pre-
vented, by these quarrels, for six months after the
proper time. Thus the Romans were not only failing
to rule their provinces justly,—as in the case of Sicily,
—but the city itself was now filled with confusion and
violence; and many wise and thoughtful men became
willing to end the disorder in any way that was possible.

At this time, Cicero was trying to cure the evils of
the government by urging the people of Rome to be
as unselfish and virtuous as their forefathers had been.
His efforts failed, for the people were not willing to
believe that their greed and selfishness were ruin-
ing their country. Perhaps, if they had believed it,
they could not have changed themselves in order to
remedy their public evils. They had no idea of alter-
ing the government by giving it the representative
form such as we have now; so the only cure that
remained was for the rule of the Senate to give way to

that of one strong man, who could put down disorder and punish wrong-doing.

But where was the strong man to be found who could, and would, force the Senate to step aside and let him carry on the government? To be able to do this, it was necessary that he should have an army, for the Senate would certainly not give up its power without a struggle. There were only two men at this time who had armies which they could use in this way. One of them was Pompey, the conqueror of the pirates and the East; the other was Cæsar, the conqueror of Gaul.

Pompey might long ago have overcome the power of the Senate, if he had really desired to do so. He did not know much about government, however, and could not make up his mind what he wanted to do. Cæsar, on the other hand, was as able in state affairs as he was in war. He had long seen that the old government was so bad that it could only be cured by setting up another in its place; and he was quite ready to undertake this himself, if the chance should come to him. For a while Cæsar and Pompey had acted together, and had helped each other in politics. But when news came to Pompey at Rome of the splendid victories which Cæsar was winning in Gaul, he began to be jealous of him, and at last he was ready to join with the party of the nobles in any plan that would destroy his power.

It had been agreed that Cæsar was to have his command in Gaul for ten years, and when that time was passed, he had arranged that he should be elected consul again. That would give him an army as consul, just as soon as he laid down the command of his army in Gaul; and when his year as consul was up, he would go to one of the provinces again as the head of another army for a long term of years. In this way there would be no time when Cæsar would not have an army at his command; and so the nobles would not be able to injure him, or put him to death, as they had Tiberius and Caius Gracchus.

The plan which the nobles and Pompey formed, to get rid of Cæsar, was this. They would make him give up his government in Gaul before his last five years were over; then, perhaps, when Cæsar had no army to protect him against injustice, they would bring him to trial before the courts at Rome on some charge —any charge would do—and have him convicted. By this means they would thrust him aside, and the selfish government of the Senate could go on as before.

To carry out this plan, the Senate ordered Cæsar to give up his governorship, and return to Rome. Cæsar knew that he could not trust himself there without an army to protect him. Nevertheless, he made an offer to the Senate to give up his command, if Pompey, who was then at Rome with an army near by, would resign his also. The Senate replied that Cæsar must give up his army, or become a traitor to his country; and that Pompey need not give up his.

Cæsar now saw that his enemies were planning to destroy him; but to resist them meant the beginning of a civil war between himself and Pompey. Nevertheless, he prepared to lead his victorious army across the little river Rubicon, which separated Cis-Alpine Gaul from Italy, and to march south upon his enemies.

The old stories say that after Cæsar had drawn up his men on the banks of the river he stood for some time in deep thought, questioning whether it was the wisest thing, after all, for him to go in arms against the government of his country. While he lingered in doubt, a wandering minstrel near by suddenly seized a trumpet from one of the soldiers and sounded the call to advance. Cæsar accepted this as a sign from the gods.

"Let us go whither the gods and the wickedness of our enemies call us," he cried. "The die is now cast." Then he led his veteran soldiers across the Rubicon and advanced to meet the army of his countrymen.

Pompey meanwhile had made almost no preparations for the war.

ROMAN SOLDIERS.

When some one had asked him what he would do if Cæsar should march upon Rome, he had replied:

"I have but to stamp my foot, and soldiers will spring up all over Italy to fill the legions of my army."

But after Cæsar had crossed the Rubicon, news was soon brought to Rome that the Italian towns were yielding to him without a struggle. When one of the senators taunted Pompey with his vain boast, and asked him why he did not stamp his foot, the latter

could find no answer. It was too late now to raise
men to save Rome; so Pompey had to leave the city
to its new master. He retreated with his army to the
south of Italy; but Cæsar promptly followed him.
Then, rather than to fight in Italy, Pompey crossed
over into Greece; for his influence was strongest there
and in the East, where his greatest victories had been
won. Cæsar could now follow him no farther, as
there were not enough ships remaining to carry his
men across the sea.

Accordingly, having driven his enemies from Italy in
sixty days, without the shedding of a drop of blood, he
turned back to Rome. There he treated the people
mildly and generously, and the men who had feared
that the terrible times of Sulla and Marius had come
again soon saw that they were mistaken. Cæsar punished no one, and he took the property of none. He
remained in the city only a short time, and then set
out for Spain, where the greatest part of Pompey's
army had been left.

"I go," he said, "to attack an army without a general; I shall return to attack a general without an
army.'

After some difficulty, Cæsar succeeded in getting
possession of the Roman provinces in Spain. He
now had Gaul, Italy, and Spain under his control, and
he could turn all his efforts against Pompey and the
forces in the East.

He led his army back through Italy by rapid
marches; and, although it was by this time the middle
of winter, he immediately crossed into Greece. Then,
for about four months, the two armies marched and

countermarched, and built camps and threw up earth-works. During all this time Pompey's army was larger than Cæsar's; and it was better fed and better cared for also, as Pompey's ships could bring him every-thing that he needed, while Cæsar's men had to live upon the country around them. Cæsar tried by every means to bring on a battle, but without success; for Pompey knew that, though he had the larger number of men, Cæsar had the better soldiers. At last, how-ever, Pompey yielded to the urging of his followers, and drew out his men for battle. The result was a great victory for Cæsar. Although Pompey had twice as large a force as the conqueror of Gaul, he was defeated and his army was destroyed.

After this battle, Pompey was forced to fly from Greece and seek refuge in Egypt. There he was basely murdered by men who wished to please Cæsar, and thought that this would be the surest way of win-ning his favor. But when Cæsar followed Pompey to Egypt, and was shown the proofs of his death, he did not rejoice, but turned away his face and wept. To all the men who had been in Pompey's army, he showed himself kind and generous; and he wrote to his friends at Rome that "the chief pleasure he had in his victory was in saving every day some one of his fellow citizens who had borne arms against him."

After Cæsar's victory over Pompey, he established his power firmly in Greece, Egypt, and Asia, as he had already done in the western countries of the Mediter-ranean. When he returned to Rome, Africa was the only portion of the Roman Empire that remained unconquered; and all who continued hostile to

Cæsar had gathered there. For a time he remained at Rome to attend to public affairs; but as soon as he could, he arranged to go to Africa and conquer this last army of his enemies.

Cæsar's soldiers, however, were wearied with marching from one end of the world to the other. The tenth legion, which had served him so well, at last rebelled, and the men demanded that they should be dismissed with the rewards that were due them for their long services. When Cæsar heard this, he went out and spoke to them.

"Citizens, you shall be dismissed as you desire," he said coldly, "and you shall have all the rewards which have been promised you."

But when the soldiers heard their beloved commander call them "citizens," instead of "fellow soldiers," as always before, they no longer desired the thing that they had asked for. The rebuke and the idea of separation, which lay in that one word, were not to be borne. They begged that they might be taken back into his service again; and after that, there was no longer any talk of dismissal on their part.

Cæsar was as successful in defeating his enemies in Africa as he had been everywhere else, and when he returned to Rome, he was able to celebrate four triumphs, one after the other, for his victories in Gaul, in Egypt, in Asia, and in Africa. On the day of his triumph over Gaul, he ascended the Capitol at night, with twenty elephants bearing torches to the right of him and twenty to the left. When he triumphed because of his victories in Asia, an inscription was carried before his chariot which read in Latin, **"I** came, I saw, I conquered.'' This was copied from a message which Cæsar had sent to the Senate announcing one of his victories, and it was intended to remind the people how quickly he had ended the troubles in the region of which he wrote.

Cæsar was now master of Rome and of her empire. The Roman army, made up of men of all countries, was the strongest power in the city; and Cæsar, who

CÆSAR'S TRIUMPH.

controlled the army, was the first man in the empire. He could now make whatever reforms in the state he thought best. As the Senate and the people had shown so plainly that they were no longer fit for the task of governing the nations under their rule, he decided to carry on the government himself. He allowed the Senate and the assemblies of the people to meet as before, but he took good care to see that they had no real power. He took charge personally of most of the public offices; and, besides the titles which went with these, he gave himself the name of "Emperor," or commander, and that in time came to be the highest title of all.

Cæsar used his great power well. Instead of treating those who had fought against him as Sulla and Marius had treated their enemies, he tried to make them his friends, and allowed them to hold offices under him. There were still some men left, united under the command of the sons of Pompey in Spain, who were determined to defy him to the last; and Cæsar was compelled to leave Rome, and lead an army against them himself before they were finally defeated. But the greater part of the people of Rome were satisfied with the rule of Cæsar, because it promised to give the peace and safety which they had not enjoyed for a long time.

Cæsar lived for only two years after the four-fold triumph which followed his return from Africa. In those two years, however, he succeeded in doing much good for Rome. He made laws for the reform of the courts of justice, and others to enable men who were in debt, and could not pay, to settle with their creditors. To reform the manners of life among the Romans he had laws passed against extravagance in dress and in banquets. He tried to check the growth of slave labor by requiring that one-third of the laborers on sheep-farms must be free. New colonies were planned to provide for the poor and idle population of the city; and he passed laws to admit many of the subjects of Rome to an equality with the citizens themselves.

Another of the changes which he carried out is of especial interest to us, because the civilized world to-day still profits by it. This was a reform of the calendar. The Romans divided the year into twelve months, as we do; but their months were not long enough, so they had an awkward way of putting in an extra month about every two years, to make the seasons come out right. This plan worked badly, and, by the time of Cæsar, the calendar and the real year of the earth's revolution around the sun, had become ninety days apart. As a result of this, the Italian farmer began his work in the fields in June and July, according to the calendar, when it was really March and April. Cæsar consulted the most learned men of his time, and the calendar was corrected and made to agree with the seasons. Then, to keep it right in the future, Cæsar increased the length of some of the months, so that the ordinary year should have three hundred and sixty-five days; and he arranged that every fourth year, or leap year, an extra day should be given to February. The calendar after this did very well, and with one small change we use it still, even retaining all the Roman names for the months. One of these, July, was given in honor of Cæsar himself, to commemorate his part in bringing the change about.

Besides these various reforms, Cæsar planned many other important works. He expected to collect a large library at Rome, and this was at a time when books were very rare and costly. A theater was also begun, and he was planning to build a new Senate house, as the old one had been burned in the terrible disorders of the late wars. A great temple to Mars was designed to keep the memory of his victories fresh in the minds of the people. At the mouth of the Tiber, an immense harbor was to be built, and a new road was projected east through the mountains to the Adriatic Sea. In the midst of all this he was preparing to lead armies against the barbarians on the Danube, and against those south of the Caspian Sea in Asia; for in both these regions the people were forcing their way out of their own lands and seeking to come into the Roman provinces.

But all these plans were left unfinished or were not even begun. Although Rome was now better off than it had been at any time for fifty years, there were some men among her citizens who still thought that there was nothing more shameful than to submit to the rule of one man. They longed for the old government of the Senate with all its faults. At last sixty of the nobles formed a plot to kill Cæsar, and so free themselves from his power in the only way that was possible. Almost all of these men had received favors from Cæsar, and one of them, Marcus Brutus, had been his friend. Brutus was not an evil man, but others who were crafty and selfish persuaded him that it was his duty to save his country from Cæsar, as his ancestor had rescued it from Tarquin long before. So, in spite of his feeling for his friend, he joined the plot and became one of its leaders.

Cæsar was warned of the danger that threatened him, but he would have no guards about him.

"It is better to die once," he said, "than to live always in fear of death."

He had been warned especially to beware of the day

which the Romans called the "Ides" of March; but on that day he went to the Senate house as usual. On the way there he saw the priest who had given him the warning; and he laughed at him, declaring him a false prophet, because the Ides of March had come and nothing had befallen him.

"The day is come, Cæsar, but it is not gone," answered the priest:

When Cæsar entered the Senate house, all the senators arose to greet him, as was their custom. Then the plotters advanced to Cæsar's chair, one of them pretending to beg a favor of him, while the rest appeared to urge the granting of this request.

Suddenly one of the plotters laid hold of Cæsar's toga, and dragged it from his shoulders. This was a signal for the others, and at once they fell upon him with their swords and daggers. For a moment Cæsar resisted them, and then he saw his friend Brutus striking at him among his foes.

"Thou, too, Brutus!" he cried, and with this he ceased his struggles. Wrapping his head in his toga, he fell, pierced with many wounds, at the foot of the statue of Pompey which stood in the Senate house.

Thus died one of the ablest men who ever lived in any country or at any time. There have been many men in the world who have been great in one way; but Cæsar was great in many ways. He was a better general, perhaps, than any man before or since his time; but he was more than this. As a writer and an orator he stood foremost among the Romans. He was a wise ruler, who saw clearly what his country needed in many different directions, and who spent the short time during which he held the power in planning reforms and improvements for her benefit. But, best of all, he had a generous and fearless spirit, and found it easy to forgive those who had injured him, and easier to die than to weakly dread to die. He was worthy to become, as he did, the first of a long line of emperors, and he left a name behind him which is even yet used as the highest of titles. When the Germans now speak of their "Kaiser," they are simply honoring their ruler by the family name of this great Roman; and even the "Czar" of the Russians is supposed to have come from the same source.

XXVI

Rome in the Time of Augustus.

THE enemies of Cæsar were able to put him to death, but they could not bring back the Republic, which he had overthrown. After he was gone, the quarrels and struggles which he had brought to an end began once more. Cæsar had left no son to succeed him, but when his will was opened it was found that he had adopted his nephew Octavius as his son, and made him his heir.

Octavius was not yet nineteen years old, but he soon showed that he possessed wisdom which was beyond his years. He accepted the inheritance, and set himself to work securing his rights under it. After many difficulties, he succeeded in this, and also in the more difficult task of punishing Cæsar's murderers, who were at last defeated and slain in battle. Then he planned to obtain Cæsar's power in the empire for himself, as the lawful successor. This was the hardest thing that he had yet attempted, for there were others who were grasping as much power as they could, and Octavius had to struggle against them. In the end, however, he succeeded in getting what he wanted. All of his rivals were disposed of, except one; then, twelve years after the death of Cæsar, Octavius won a great battle over this man, and became master of the whole Roman world.

AUGUSTUS CÆSAR.

For a hundred years—ever since the time of the Gracchi—the party of the people and the party of the nobles had been contending together, but neither one could find a cure for the troubles that filled the Roman lands. The world was now worn out with these struggles. The time had come when both the nobles and the people must finally yield to the rule of one man, with an army to carry out his commands. In this way alone could peace, order, and happiness be brought to the millions of people who were in the power of Rome. Octavius established the rule of the empire, which Cæsar had begun; and he established it so firmly that it lasted undisturbed for five hundred years after him. From the time when Octavius obtained the power, there was no longer any dispute as to what form of government there should be; the only question was, who should be the one to carry on the government under the form which had been given to it.

When Octavius became emperor he called himself "Augustus," and it is by this name that we must now speak of him. He was a good ruler, and during the many years that he governed the empire, the world about the Mediterranean was happier than it had ever been before. The doors of the temple of Janus, which had been shut only three times since Rome was founded, were now closed again during long periods; for peace—"the Roman peace," as it was proudly called—was spread over the world. From Spain to Greece, from Gaul to Egypt, there was no longer any war. Travelers came and went in safety on the great roads with which the Romans had covered the world; the farmers sowed and reaped their fields in peace, and the merchants sent out their goods by land and sea with no cause to fear that an enemy might rob them of their gains.

Augustus decided that the empire was now as large as it ought ever to become. He fixed the rivers Rhine and Danube as the boundaries, on the north, beyond which the Romans should not seek to rule; and he caused a chain of forts to be built along these rivers to defend the Roman lands against the attacks of the wild tribes who lived beyond. Nearly all the emperors who came after Augustus accepted these limits. Almost the only land that was added to the empire after this time was the island of Britain, and Julius Cæsar had already prepared the way for its conquest while he was overcoming Gaul.

At Rome, Augustus had many new temples built, and those of the older ones, that were showing signs of age and use, he caused to be repaired and covered over with a facing of marble. Before he died, he could say, in speaking of this work:

"I found Rome built of brick, but I leave it built of marble."

Augustus was also fond of encouraging and rewarding poets and other writers. Partly because of this there were more great literary men at Rome during his time than ever before or after; and for this reason whenever we wish to describe a period which is remarkable for many great writers, we still call it an "Augustan age."

It is from these writers of the reign of Augustus that we learn some of the most interesting things about the life of the Roman people. If we wish to see the citi-

TOGA—FRONT.

zens in their streets and homes, instead of upon the battlefield as so often heretofore, we have now only to imagine ourselves the companions for a day of the poet Horace, who was one of the wisest and wittiest writers of the time.

For this glimpse of the city in the peaceful reign of Augustus, it will be well to choose a day when there is no great festival or show, in order that we may see the ordinary life of the people. The Romans keep early hours, so we must be up before sunrise and make our way to the modest home of Horace on the hill that lies east of the Forum. There we find the poet risen and dressed for the street, though he is usually later than most of his neighbors. To-day, however, he is going to pay a morning visit to his friend Mæcenas, and he is up in good time.

After a light breakfast of bread dipped in wine, and ripe olives, we set out together. As we pass along the narrow streets, we are surprised at the number of people that we meet, though the sun is barely up above the horizon. Some are slaves and servants, hurrying here and

TOGA—BACK.

there on business of their masters. Others are children on their way to school, with slaves accompanying them, and carrying their tablets and satchels. Many, however, are freemen, and are clad in the toga, which none but a free Roman citizen may wear. These bustle along with little baskets in their hands and anxious looks upon their faces. They are "clients," we are told, or dependants of great men, who are hurrying to pay their visit of state to their patron at his morning reception; and the little baskets are to carry away the gifts of food which are set out for them each day in their patron's house.

As we approach the splendid mansion of Mæcenas, with its beautiful gardens, we see many of these clients going into the house before us; and as we enter we find the outer hall and vestibule full of them. Mæcenas is the friend and adviser of Augustus, and his influence in the state is very great. As he is also a liberal and kindly man, the number of clients who are dependent on him is quite large. However, we are not troubled by the number of these visitors, though they are pushing and shoving to get ahead of one another; for Horace is upon quite a different footing with Mæcenas, and is admitted at once to the presence of the master of the house.

We enter with him, and find ourselves in a large stately hall, richly ornamented with pictures and statues. There Mæcenas is receiving the greetings of the more important of his clients, while he advises one, perhaps, on some point connected with a suit at law, and tells another how best to invest his money. But as soon as he sees Horace, he comes forward with a smile on his face, for he loves him, and honors him as Rome's greatest poet. While the two friends talk, we glance about the hall, and admire the graceful marble columns which support the roof. From time to time we catch bits of the conversation between Mæcenas and our guide.

"Nay, Mæcenas," Horace is saying, "though no one is of a nobler family than yourself, you are not one of those who toss up their heads at men of humble birth. If you had been such a person, I should have had no chance of ever gaining your friendship and aid; for my father, as you know, was born a slave, though he gained his freedom. I shall never be ashamed of my father, however, for though he was a poor man on a lean little farm, he guarded me from bad habits and gave me an education fit for a senator's son."

After some further talk, Horace takes his leave, and we return with him to his little home. As we enter we glance at a sun-dial which stands near by, and see that it is near the close of the second hour, or about eight o'clock.

In the Forum, the next three hours are the busiest of the day. Now the judges are seated on their benches, listening to the pleas of the orators in the suits at law; and now the crowd of idlers is greatest there. But Horace is not interested in such matters; he quietly enters his library, and there he remains, reading and writing, until near midday. Then, a light luncheon of bread, cold meat, fruit, and wine is served by the slaves; and after that comes the midday rest and nap, which is still common in all warm climates.

In the afternoon, we accompany Horace, once more, as he leaves the house and sets out for the heart of the city. As we stroll along, we see groups of children gathered in the shadow of the houses. Here some girls are playing a game with small bones, which is very much like our "jack stones," and others sit singing to their dolls. Elsewhere we find groups of active boys, playing with nuts in much the same ways that our boys play with marbles.

As we pass the shops where provisions are sold, Horace stops to ask the prices of herbs and bread of the slaves, who have the shops in charge; and when he comes to the booth of a fortune teller, he stands listening in the crowd for a while, and smiles at the silly folk who believe all the nonsense that is told them. When we reach the Forum, we find it almost deserted; only a few laggards, like ourselves, are to be seen, and they seem to be on their way toward the open ground by the river.

We follow after them, and soon reach the Field of Mars. Here the armies assemble in time of war, and here, too, we see the voting places where the elections are held each year. But it is nothing of this sort that draws the people now. As we look about us, we see everywhere men of all ages—old and young—engaged in games and exercises of some sort; and almost every afternoon, at this time, we could find the same sight. Men are running, leaping, wrestling, hurling the spear and quoit. Some are practicing feats on horseback; others, armed with shields and stout clubs, are aiming heavy blows at tall posts; and others still are playing games with balls of various kinds and sizes.

For a while Horace takes part in this latter exercise. We join him and throw the ball about until our muscles are tired and our bodies heated with the exercise in the bright sunshine. Then, leaving the Field of Mars, we go to refresh ourselves at the baths.

To the Roman, the daily bath is just as important as daily exercise; and many fine and costly buildings, for this purpose, have been erected by wealthy men and opened to the people. Some of these include within them gardens, columned porches, libraries, and everything that can give one comfort and amusement; and these baths have come to be great places of resort for the Roman idlers.

We will go with Horace, however, to one of the less pretentious buildings, where baths alone are to be found. There, for a very small sum, we may have a cold swimming bath, a hot-water or a hot-air bath. We make our choice, and after bathing, and rubbing our bodies with olive oil, we are delightfully refreshed and ready to enjoy the remainder of the day.

Horace has been invited to dinner, for this evening, at the house of an acquaintance. The water-clocks and sun-dials tell us that it is now nearing the ninth hour,—by our time about three o'clock—so we must hasten, as Roman dinners begin in the middle of the afternoon. When we reach the house, we are at once shown into the dining-room. There we find the little company gathered, and among them we recognize Mæcenas, whose reception we attended in the early morning. Standing with him, we see a man of fine features and bright eyes, whose face lights up as, now and then, in the course of the conversation, he quotes a verse of poetry. This is Vergil, the friend of Horace, whose great poem on the fall of Troy has been preserved, and is yet read with delight by scholars the world over.

In the center of the room we see a small table of maple wood, and about three sides of this are arranged couches or sofas on which the guests are to recline during the dinner. When we have taken our places, three on a couch, slaves advance and remove the sandals from our feet. Others hand around silver basins filled with water, for our hands, which ceases to surprise us when we notice that there are no knives or forks upon the table to serve in place of fingers.

VERGIL.

When our hands have been bathed and dried, slaves enter with a tray containing the first course of the dinner. This is placed on the table in front of us, and we see that it consists of a wild boar roasted whole, with eggs, lettuce, radishes, olives, and other relishes heaped about it. While we are being helped to these dishes, wine mixed with honey is handed about in golden goblets. After this course many others follow,—roast fowls, fresh oysters, fish with strange sauces, blackbirds roasted with their feathers on, pastry made in wonderful shapes, fruits and nuts. Yet this is not a fine banquet, according to their ideas; for whole fortunes, at times, are spent by the Romans on a single entertainment.

Though we took our places at the table at three o'clock, we do not rise from it until near sunset. After the hunger of all is satisfied, basins of water are again passed for the cleansing of the hands after the repast. But the guests still linger about the table, drinking wine weakened with water, playing at games, and talking.

As we listen to the conversation our attention is caught by something that Horace is saying. He is expressing his preference for a life in the country, and declaring how much he would rather be at his little farm near Rome, which the generous Mæcenas has given him, than in the bustling city.

"Happy is the man," he says, "who tills his little farm with his own oxen, far away from the noise and hurry of the city. He is neither alarmed by the trumpet which calls the soldier to arms, nor frightened by the storms which cause the merchant to fear for his ships at sea. In the spring he trims his vines, stores his honey, and shears his sheep; and when autumn comes, he gathers his pears and the purple grape. He may lie full length on the matted grass under some old tree, and listen to the warbling of the birds in the woods, and the waters gliding by in their deep channels. And when winter comes, with its rains and snows, he may hunt the wild boar with his hounds, or spread nets to take thrushes, and snares to catch hares and cranes."

At last the company breaks up, just as the sun is setting beyond the Tiber. All the company go to their homes, for as the Romans are early risers, they go to bed early also. Soon after darkness has fallen, the greater part of the people in this vast city are buried in slumber, while the shadows of the streets are only broken, here and there, by a glimmer from the lamp of some belated household. The Roman day is at an end.

XXVII

The Empire After Augustus.

WHEN Augustus died, the whole empire mourned for him. As time went on, however, men regretted him yet more bitterly; for it was long before they had another ruler as wise and good.

The step-son of Augustus became emperor after him, and he was a cruel tyrant who put men to death upon mere suspicion. The next emperor was half-mad, and once threatened to have his horse made consul. At another time he raised a great army, and marched it hundreds of miles, only to command the soldiers to gather the shells upon the sea-beach and carry them back to Rome. After him came a weak and foolish emperor who allowed the cruelest acts to be committed in his name, and immediately forgot them, and invited the persons to dinner whom he had just caused to be put to death. Then came an emperor named Nero, who was a monster of vanity and cruelty. He was suspected of setting fire to the city and allowing more than two-thirds of it to burn, in order that he might rebuild it finer than it had been before.

But even under such rulers, the misgovernment scarcely extended beyond the city of Rome itself, and the distant provinces were more prosperous and happy than they had been during the time when the Senate and the people of Rome ruled over them. For a hundred years there was no civil war. Then when one did begin, after the death of Nero, it lasted only a short time, and ended by bringing in a succession of emperors, almost every one of whom was as strong and worthy as Augustus.

Before this civil war, all the emperors who had ruled had been related in some way to the family of Julius Cæsar; but after it, this was no longer the case. The emperors now were usually the leaders of the armies which guarded the different borders of the empire. Like the soldiers whom they commanded, they were often not Romans at all, but had been born and reared in some of the provinces. They did not care so much for the city of Rome and the Romans, therefore; and in the course of time the people of Sicily and Spain, and finally of all the provinces, were admitted to have equal rights in the empire with the citizens of Rome itself.

A new plan was found in this period for providing a successor for the ruler of the empire. The emperor would choose the best man he could find, and adopt him as his son; then this son would share the rule with him while he lived, and succeed him when he died. In this way the empire had a hundred years of the best government that it was ever to know. Indeed, the people who dwell about the Mediterranean have never experienced since a time of such unbroken happiness.

One of the emperors who made this period famous was named Trajan, and he became so great a favorite, that when the Romans wished to pay a compliment to a ruler after this, they could only declare him to be "more fortunate than Augustus and better than Trajan." He was a fine general, and made war upon the people who lived beyond the Danube, conquering some of their territory; but this was soon given up again. To celebrate his victories, Trajan set up in the Forum at Rome, a carved marble column, one hundred and thirty feet high, with his statue on the top. This column still stands after eighteen hundred years; and winding around the outside of it may yet be traced carvings of scenes from his wars about the Danube.

Trajan was followed by the Emperor Hadrian, a man of peace, and a great traveler and builder. He visited all the provinces of the empire, from far-off Britain to Egypt and the East. Wherever he went he caused new temples, theaters, and other public buildings to be raised, and the old ones to be repaired. In Britain, he built a great wall across the island from sea to sea, to protect the Roman citizens there against the tribes that lived in what is now Scotland.

The two emperors who came just after Hadrian were

different from any that had gone before. They were
scholars and wise men, and liked the quiet of their
libraries much better than the noise of armies and
battles, or the traveling of which Hadrian had been so
fond. But they both governed with the single purpose of making the people under their rule as happy
as possible; so when it became necessary to make war
to defend the empire, they
did not hesitate to give up
their own desires and march
at the head of their armies.
This became more and more
necessary during the reign of
Marcus Aurelius, the second
of these two emperors; and
finally he met his death on
the bank of the River Danube, fighting against the Germans who lived along that
stream.

With the death of this
great and good ruler, the
"golden age" of the empire

MARCUS AURELIUS.

came to an end. From now on the barbarians pressed
more closely on the northern boundaries, and it became
more difficult to repel their attacks. The Romans and
the Italians had lost their former courage and skill in
fighting, which had enabled them to conquer the whole
world; while the barbarians had learned much about war
from their long struggles with Rome. Besides this, the
government now fell once more into unworthy hands.
Ignorant soldiers gave the rule to men who were not fit

for it; and at one time the position of emperor was even put up at auction and sold to the highest bidder.

So a hundred years of war and bloodshed followed. This did not cease, until at last a strong ruler named Diocletian got the power, and divided the empire into an eastern and western half, each with its own ruler, so that the people might be better defended from the barbarians, and better governed in their own countries. Many other changes were made by Diocletian; then when his work was finished, he resigned his power and spent the rest of his days in quiet, far from the struggles of war and politics.

Soon after Diocletian had laid down his power, a new emperor ruled who once more united the eastern and western halves of the empire. This emperor, Constantine the Great, did two very important things. He was the first emperor to become a Christian himself, and to allow the Christians to practice their religion openly, and he moved the capital of the Roman empire to the shores of the Black Sea, where he built a new city which was called "Constantinople," or "the city of Constantine." Some time after the death of Constantine the empire was again divided into an eastern and a western part; and this time the division was a lasting one. After that there was an empire of the east, with its capital at Constantinople; and an empire of the west, with its capital at Rome.

Meanwhile, the barbarians, especially the Germans, had been growing more and more troublesome. Great hordes of them at last broke through the line of forts along the Rhine and the Danube, and wandered up and down the lands of the empire, plundering and destroying for many years. Battle after battle was fought with them, and sometimes the Germans were the victors, and sometimes the Romans; but the armies of the emperors were never again strong enough to drive them out of the Roman lands.

Then the Romans tried to buy off the Germans by giving them districts in which to settle, and by taking their young men into the Roman armies. But the news of the success of these bands soon brought others after them, all demanding lands within the bounds of the empire. Often they would not wait to request a place to settle, but would seize upon it without asking, and the armies of the empire could not hinder them. In this way, Spain, Gaul, Britain, and even northern Italy, passed into the hands of the Germans; and in all these lands the Roman rule came to an end forever.

In the east the new city of Constantinople was so well situated, and so strongly built, that the Germans were never able to capture it; and the empire there went on for a thousand years longer. But the empire of the west was not so strong. The city of Rome had been greatly weakened when Constantine moved the capital to the Black Sea, and it was not so able to withstand the attacks of the barbarians. Just eight hundred years after it had first been taken by the Gauls, Rome fell into the hands of the barbarians a second time, and was plundered by a wandering tribe of Germans. Then sixty-six years later, in the year 476 after Christ, one of these German chiefs seized the last Roman emperor in Italy, and took his crown and scepter from him; and the Roman empire of the west quietly came to an end.

So the vast territory of Rome had shrunken again to the city itself. The Romans had gained their power in the beginning because they were worthy to rule, and they lost it when they were no longer capable of doing so. The rule of Rome, which had at first been a blessing to the world, at last became an injury to it; and when that time came, it was easy for the Germanic barbarians to overthrow the old government.

But it is easier to destroy an empire than it is to create one. The Germans were at this time a rude and unlettered people, who had never lived in cities and were ignorant of many things connected with ruling over them. It was to take them a long time to learn to govern as well as the old Romans had done, but in the end they succeeded in doing so. Then the modern nations of Europe arose out of the ruins of the Roman Empire, and united in themselves all that was best of the old Roman civilization, with the newer and freer ideas of the Germans.

XXVIII

The Christians and the Empire.

DURING the centuries while the Roman power was slowly passing away, another was gathering strength to take its place. This was the Christian religion, which took possession of the minds and hearts of the Romans; then of the barbarian Germans, who had conquered them; and so spread about the world and overcame it in a better way than that of Rome.

Palestine, the land of the Jews, was first conquered by Pompey, before his war with Cæsar, while he was setting the affairs of the east in order. There Christ was born while Augustus was emperor, and he was put to death in the reign of the successor of Augustus. Up to that time the teachings of Christ had not spread beyond the groups of Jews who had accepted them. After his death, however, the Apostles—especially the Apostle Paul—began to carry his message to other nations; and soon there were little bands of Christians to be found in many of the cities about the Mediterranean Sea.

Then it began to be a question as to how the Roman government would treat this new religion. Usually the Romans were very tolerant, and allowed the nations that they conquered to worship whatever gods they chose, and even to establish their religion in

Rome itself. The Egyptians and Jews and other eastern nations had been allowed to build temples in the capitol, and worship their gods there with almost no hindrance or disturbance.

It was different, however, with the Christians. There were many reasons why the Romans would not let them worship freely. The Jews were very bitter against the Christians, and they informed the Romans that the new sect were guilty of many horrible crimes in their meetings. These charges were not true, of course; but the Romans, and the Jews themselves, believed them. Then, too, the Christians were charged with introducing a new and strange god, and with denying that the gods of the empire were gods at all. They would not offer sacrifice to the Roman deities—especially to the statues of the emperors, who were now looked upon as gods. So they were charged with rebellion, and with plotting to overthrow the government; and whenever war, or famine, or disease, came upon the people, they were ready to blame it upon the Christians.

"The gods are angry with us for sheltering those who deny them!" they cried at such times. "The Christians must be put to death! To the lions with the Christians!"

Then all persons who were suspected of holding the new faith were seized and hurried off to the judges. If they admitted that they were Christians, they were promptly sentenced to death. If they denied it, they were asked to offer sacrifice to the statue of the emperor. In case they refused, the charge was regarded as proved, and they, too, were declared guilty.

In this way the prisons were filled with Christians. It made no difference whether they were slave or free, old or young, strong men or delicate women,—their fate was the same. When next the people were gathered to see the games in the great Circus, the Christians were driven into the arena. Then lions, and leopards were turned loose upon them, while the cruel Romans shouted and cheered from their seats above.

The first persecution of the Christians at Rome took place while Nero was emperor. A great fire had broken out, burning more than two-thirds of the city; and, as has been said, the Romans blamed this upon their reckless emperor. It was reported that while the waves of flame were sweeping over the city, Nero had been seen on a tower, watching the sight, and carelessly playing upon a harp and singing. The Roman people were very angry, and for a while a rebellion seemed to be threatened. To quiet them, Nero had it reported that it was the Christians who had started the fire, and that while it was burning many of them had been seen going about with torches in their hands, lighting the buildings which had not yet caught.

This turned the people's wrath from their emperor to the Christians. The cry arose on every side, "To the lions with the Christians"; and hundreds of them were hurried off to prison without any kind of trial. Nero also invented many new and cruel punishments for them. Some were covered with the skins of wild beasts, and dogs were set on them. Others were wrapped in sheets of pitch and burned at night in the emperor's gardens, under the name of Nero's candles. Others, more mercifully, were put to death in their prisons; and in later days it was said that the Apostles Peter and Paul had been called upon to end their lives thus.

It was not always, however, the evil emperors like Nero who persecuted the Christians. Sometimes the worst treatment was given them by the orders of good emperors, who were ignorant of the real teachings of Christ, and believed that the charges made against the sect were true. In this way it happened that Trajan, Marcus Aurelius, and Diocletian all persecuted the Christians, and had large numbers of them put to death. These troubles lasted for such a great length of time that for generations they were forced to worship in secret and have a refuge that should be always ready when danger threatened.

One of the great differences between the Christians and the Romans was in the disposal of their dead. Instead of burning the bodies in the Roman fashion, the Christians buried them; but not in cemeteries such as we know. They dug out great tunnels and caves in the soft rock, and formed tombs along the sides of these. In the course of years the hills of Rome came to be mined through and through with such tunnels, or "catacombs," as they were called. They made a great network of passages, miles and miles in length, which crossed and re-crossed one another, under the city, just as the Roman streets did on the surface of the ground above. When a persecution began, the Christians would hide themselves in these streets of the dead beneath the town; and there, too, they would often hold their church services to comfort and support one another in their times of trial and distress.

In spite of the protection of the catacombs, many hundreds of Christians were put to death because of their religion; and many more were imprisoned, or suffered in other ways for their faith. These were called "martyrs," which means "witnesses" for the Truth. Some of the most earnest Christians eagerly sought to receive a martyr's death, and mourned if they were not granted it. Even boys and girls became heroes in these persecutions, and endured death without flinching,—glad that they were suffering as Christ had suffered for them.

One of the noblest martyrs of this time was a man named Polycarp, who was put to death in Asia Minor while Marcus Aurelius was emperor. He was then an old man of ninety years, and all the Christians of the east looked up to him with love and admiration, for he had been a disciple of the Apostle John. When the soldiers came to arrest him, their commander took pity on him, and tried to persuade him to sacrifice to the Roman gods, and so save his life.

"What harm can there be in saying 'the emperor, our Lord,' and in offering sacrifices to him?" he asked.

At first Polycarp was silent; but when they went on to urge him, he said mildly:

"I will not do as you advise me."

When he was brought before the Roman governor of that province, he, too, urged him to swear by the emperor as by a god, and give proof of his repentance by saying, with the people, "Away with the godless." But Polycarp looked with a firm eye at the crowd that stood by; then pointing directly at them and with his eyes lifted to heaven, he cried:

"Away with the godless."

The governor urged him further, however. "Curse Christ, and I will release you," he said.

"Eighty-six years have I served him," answered Polycarp. "He has done me nothing but good,—and how could I curse him, my Lord and Saviour? If you wish to know what I am, I tell you frankly I am a Christian."

Even then the Roman governor wished to save the brave old man, but Polycarp would not yield. At last a herald proclaimed his faith to the assembled people.

"Polycarp has confessed that he is a Christian."

When the people heard these words, they cried out that he was the father of the Christians, that he was the enemy of their gods, and that he had taught many to turn from their worship and cease to sacrifice in their temples. They demanded that Polycarp should be burned at the stake, and they themselves gathered the wood from the workshops and the baths. Then the Roman governor was obliged to give his consent, and Polycarp met his death with the same steadfastness and courage which he had shown at his trial.

Men and women of all classes and of all ages suffered thus and were put to death, but still the number of the Christians increased with each persecution.

"Go on," said one of the Christian writers to the Roman rulers; "go on,—torture us and grind us to dust. Our numbers increase more rapidly than you mow us down. The blood of the martyrs is the seed of the Church."

At last the time came when the persecutions ceased altogether, and the emperors themselves, and all of their officers became Christians. This happened, as you have already learned, while Constantine was on the throne. During the first part of his reign the emperor had to struggle against several rivals for his power. At one time, the story goes, while he was marching rapidly from Gaul into Italy to attack one of his enemies, he saw a flaming cross in the sky, in broad daylight, and on the cross were these words:

"In this sign, conquer."

In the battle which followed, Constantine did conquer; and he believed that he owed his victory to the god of the Christians. So immediately afterwards he issued an order to stop the persecutions and permit the Christians to practice their religion openly and in peace.

After this, Constantine became a Christian himself, and did all that he could to favor their cause. Temples were taken away from the priests of the old gods and given to the Christians to use as churches; and only Christians were appointed to offices under the empire. When Constantine died, his sons remained in the same faith; and the number of the Christians grew rapidly under them. The nephew of Constantine, however, ceased to be a Christian when he became emperor, and tried to bring the people back to the worship of Mars and Jupiter once more, but he did not succeed. The new faith had taken too deep a hold on the hearts of the people. After him, all of the emperors were Christians; and at last a time came when the old worship was done away with altogether. The altars of the gods were thrown down; their images were broken; and the sacred fire in the temple of Vesta, which had burned without interruption for eleven centuries, was extinguished forever. The new religion was firmly established and had already begun to change the world.

XXIX

The Remains of Rome.

THE Roman Empire came to an end many centuries ago, but much of what its people were and did still remains. The Romans live for us yet in their history, and also in the languages and laws of Europe, which are founded in large part upon the language and law of Rome. Their roads, bridges, and walls can even now be traced all over Europe, and at Rome a few great buildings remain which give us a faint idea of the grandeur of the ancient city. Moreover, by a strange chance, the Roman city of Pompeii has been preserved for us entire, very much as it was toward the close of the first century after Christ; and in this we can draw near to the life of the people of Rome as it must have been eighteen hundred years ago.

You will remember that the earlier Romans of the time of Cincinnatus lived partly in the country upon their farms, and partly in the city. Although the Romans of the empire had changed greatly in their thoughts and tastes from those of the earlier days, they were like them in this,—that they did not confine themselves to a life in Rome. Every citizen who was able to afford it, had a house outside the city, on some beautiful Italian lake, at the foot of the mountains, or on the seashore. The western coast of Italy was lined, in places, with the country houses, or villas, of the Romans; and one beautiful bay—that on which the city of Naples stands—was noted for the number of the towns and villas around its shores.

Overlooking this bay, at the present time, is the lofty peak of Mt. Vesuvius. Travelers who visit the city of Naples to-day are sometimes fortunate enough to see an eruption of Vesuvius; for it is now one of the most active volcanoes of the world. Up to the first century after Christ, however, the Romans knew nothing of Vesuvius as an active volcano. Cities were built at its very foot; and one of the Roman writers describes it as rising behind these towns, "well cultivated and inhabited all around, except the top, which is for the most part level and entirely barren, ashy to the view, and displaying great hollows in rocks which look as if they had been eaten by fire. So we may suppose this spot," he continues, "to have been a volcano formerly, with burning craters, which are now extinguished for want of fuel."

In the year 79 A.D., the fires of Vesuvius burst forth again, after their long quiet, and brought destruction to the country around it. It was the afternoon of a November day, and the burning heats of summer were past. Many of the Roman visitors had left their country homes, and returned to the capital. Some, however, still lingered in their beautiful villas; and such of them as were not taking their afternoon nap were reading, or busying themselves with other matters. In the cities near by, life was going on as usual. In one place masons were at work repairing a damaged building, while the shopkeepers were showing their wares to customers in the Forum, and in the crowded theater men and women watched with eager faces the struggles of the gladiators.

Suddenly a strange cloud, shaped like a pine-tree, with a lofty trunk and a cluster of branches at the top, was seen to rise above Vesuvius. As the people watched, it continually changed in height; and was sometimes bright as fire and sometimes streaked with black.

This was the beginning of a great eruption of dust and ashes, which lasted for days, and is said to have scattered its showers of volcanic dust as far as Africa and Egypt. At the same time, the land was shaken by earthquakes and the sea drew back from the shore. In terror, the people fled in all directions, by sea and land, thinking the end of the world had come. Most of them escaped in safety, but some, who tried to brave the danger and remain in the cities, were lost.

When the eruption had ceased, it was found that a thick layer of ashes and mud was spread over the country around, and the towns which were nearest to the mountain were covered so deeply that only the tops of the tallest buildings were visible above the surface of the ground. As the years went by, other eruptions came, and added to the thickness of this covering. Then the top layer was gradually changed to a fine loam and vegetation sprang up and covered the spot where the cities lay buried. At last they seemed wholly lost to the memory of man.

For sixteen hundred years the towns about Mount Vesuvius remained securely hidden. Then a well, deeper than usual, happened to be dug above one of them, and ancient statues were unearthed, and bits of sculptured marble.   Search was made, and it was found that the well had struck the stage of a buried theater.   Then scholars remembered the story of the destruction of the cities so long ago, and they began to dig elsewhere.

From that time to this, the work of uncovering the buried cities has been slowly progressing.   Several museums are now filled with the pictures, statues, and household furniture which have been taken from beneath the ashes of Vesuvius.   The town which has been most thoroughly examined is Pompeii, of which over one-half has been laid bare.   There we of the twentieth century can see the houses and streets of the first century after Christ, very much as they were left when the citizens fled in fear for their lives through the showers of falling stones and ashes.

The removal of the earth over Pompeii has shown that the city had a forum, surrounded by temples and law courts, and other public buildings; and this, as at Rome, was the most splendid part of the city. It is not for the public buildings, however, that we care most: ancient temples, and other public buildings, as well preserved as these, may be found in other places.   But the glimpse which we get here into the private houses of the town, and into the life of the people in the streets and shops, we can get nowhere else, and it is this which makes our interest in Pompeii so great.

The first thing that strikes the traveler who is viewing the town for the first time is the narrowness of the streets.   In some of the broadest of them, two chariots could scarcely have passed each other; and some of

the ways are so narrow as not even to allow the
entrance of one. The pavements are formed of large
pieces of stone, joined together with great care; and
the ruts worn by the passing wheels can still be seen
in some of them. On each side of the street is a narrow walk for the foot passengers. This is raised above
the level of the roadway, and large stepping-stones are

A STREET IN POMPEII.

placed in the middle of the street to enable the people
to cross from one side to the other in rainy weather.

The houses along these cramped streets are placed
out to the edge of the pavement, and have their plain
and unadorned side toward the passers-by. They are
built,—as are the houses in many countries to-day,—
about one or more inner courts into which most of the

rooms open. Often the street side was occupied by shops which were rented out by the owner and which had no connection with the life of the house itself.

Upon entering even one of the finest of these dwelling houses, the visitor goes through a passageway lying between two of the shops which make up the front of the house. On the floor of this entry there is likely to be the Latin word for "Welcome" formed of bits of stone in Mosaic work. Crossing this, one enters first the large public reception hall. Here the master of the house received the visitors who came to see him on business, or to pay their respects to him. If they came from a distance, they might have been lodged over night in the small rooms which open off from the hall on each side. The walls of this large room were decorated with paintings and drawings, and here and there are pedestals where statues once stood. The floor here, and, indeed, all through the lower story of the house, was formed of blocks of marble or other stone, and usually these were selected of different colors and were arranged to form a pattern of some sort.

In the center of the floor of this main room is a square basin, several feet deep, which lay just beneath a corresponding opening in the roof and caught the rain which fell through it. Unfortunately, the roofs of the houses have all been broken down or burned, and the rooms are now open to the sky; but we know of this arrangement from many other sources. In the beginning, it was left to let out the smoke and vapors from the fires; for none of the houses had chimneys, and the fireplaces were only metal pots or pans in which charcoal might be burned. We could not imagine ourselves living, during our colder winters, with such an opening over our heads; but in the warm climate of Italy, this plan had many advantages. For one thing, the rooms were thus freely ventilated; and an awning, drawn across the opening, served to keep out the sun in summer.

Leaving the public hall, the visitor comes through

A ROMAN HOUSE.

another passage to the private part of the house, where the women and children lived, and where no guest might enter without a special invitation from the master. Here is another court, with rows of slender, graceful columns about it. Opening from this are small low bedrooms, which we should think very uncomfortable; and here, too, is the dining-room, where the master of the house entertained his friends at dinner. Above this court, also, there was an opening in the roof, with a basin below to catch the water; and about the basin and among the columns, there perhaps grew beds of blooming flowers and clumps of evergreens.

Only the ground floor remains of most of the houses of Pompeii; but there must have been a second story to all of the better houses, and sometimes even a third. But the upper part of the house was for the use of the slaves and the dependants of the family, and could not have been so well arranged, nor so beautiful, as the lower floor.

At the first discovery of such a house as this the walls were not found hung with framed pictures, as with us. Instead of that, they were beautifully decorated with designs and scenes painted on the wall itself, the colors still almost fresh in the darkness of the buried city. Some of these pictures have now been allowed to fade by exposure to the light and air; but a number of them have been carefully taken down and preserved in the museums.

When these houses were first uncovered, many pieces of furniture remained in them; although according to our ideas, the Roman rooms must have seemed rather bare for comfort. We should have found only a few chairs, some small tables, three couches in the dining-room, some beds or couches in the bedrooms, and here and there high stands for their queer oil lamps. The form of these articles, however, was often most graceful; and at times they were made of rich material and with great skill of workmanship. Besides such larger pieces of furniture, numerous smaller articles have been found, as the work of unearthing the city has gone on, —among them cooking vessels, vases, cups, and fine glasses, combs, hairpins, polished metal mirrors, and pieces of jewelry.

The shops of Pompeii are as interesting as the private houses. Most of these are only small rooms in the front of the houses, and are entirely open toward the street. Usually each shop displays a sign; the milk store, a wooden goat, and the wine shop a large jar. A snake before another shop shows that it has been a drug store, and a row of hams is the sign of an eating house. Three bakeries have been discovered, and these give us some idea of how the bread of the

SPOONS FROM POMPEII.

Romans looked; for in the oven of one of them, eighty-three loaves were discovered, black and charred, but still keeping their original shape. A washing and dyeing shop has also been found, for the

DRINKING BOWL FROM POMPEII.

care of the woolen garments which were almost the only kind worn. There the stone tubs may still be seen waiting for their contents, while on the walls are pictures of men standing in them and stamping with their feet, to show how they were used in washing garments.

In one way the people of Pompeii were very much like some thoughtless boys of our own day. They loved to scratch and write on the walls of the houses of the town,—which, indeed, must have offered tempting chances to all by being out upon the sidewalk.

LAMP AND STAND.

So here we find verses from the poets; and there, letters of the Greek alphabet, written by boys too small to reach high up on the walls. In many places advertisements are scratched in the plastering, and announcements of gladiator fights, and performances in the theater. Occasionally, too, we find comic pictures such as the one in which a gladiator is seen coming down the steps of the amphitheater, with a palm leaf of victory in his right hand. Such drawings and inscriptions are often found on the ancient buildings of Rome also. There, as at Pompeii, they must have been the work of the common people and the young boys, for the writers are usually very uncertain of their grammar and spelling.

The old Roman life has been kept for us better in the city of Pompeii than anywhere else; for at Rome itself, the buildings, furniture, tools, and ornaments changed with the passing centuries. People continued to live in the greater city and their personal belongings varied with the customs of the different ages. Now only a few great monuments of the past remain among them; though one who did not know the later history of Rome might wonder how the magnificent buildings of the older town, solidly built of stone and marble, could have been so nearly destroyed, even in such a long space of time.

For many hundreds of years after the Roman empire of the west had come to an end, the people of the city knew little of the past, and cared still less about it. They used the old temples for churches, changing them to suit their purposes; and they tore down the finest buildings of the older city, in order to get stone for use in building new ones of their own. There is no doubt that, in this way, the Romans themselves have done more harm to the old city than all the armies that have ever captured it. If we could only learn

CAMPANI VICTORIA VNA
CVMNVCERINIS PERISTIS

DRAWING ON THE OUTER WALL OF
A HOUSE IN POMPEII.

the history and the former use of each of the marbles, stones, and bricks, of which the palaces and churches of modern Rome are built, our knowledge of the city of the Cæsars would be almost complete.

In the fifteenth century the Church of St. Peter, the grandest in the world to-day, was begun at Rome, and rose slowly for more than two hundred years before it reached completion. The building of this church alone caused more destruction to the remains of ancient Rome than the ten centuries of ignorance that had gone before. Of the huge masses of marble of every color and size used in it, not an inch was dug from the quarries in modern times. They were all taken from the ancient buildings, many of which were leveled to the ground for the sake of one or two pieces only. At this time, also, the greatest sculptors that Italy has ever seen were flourishing; and they too found marbles ready to their hand in the fallen columns of the ancient temples. In this way, the materials of the most beautiful Christian chapel in the world were taken from the tomb of Emperor Hadrian.

If you ever go to Rome, and see the great arching dome of St. Peter's, and the other beautiful sights of the modern city, you must remember this. The new Rome which the eye sees contains the Rome of ancient times beneath its soil and in its greatest buildings, in something of the same way in which our language holds the old Latin words, changed into a different form, and put to fresh uses in our speech. At first glance we see only that which is new, and we think that the old has completely perished; but, as we learn more and are able to see more clearly, we find that the past is also there.

SUMMARIES OF CHAPTERS.

I.—The Peninsula of Italy.

1. Position, size, and shape; comparison with Greece and Spain.
2. Climate.
3. Surface: the valley of the River Po; the Apennine mountains; the plains.
4. Rivers: general character; the River Tiber.
5. Coast lands: in the northwest; about the mouth of the Tiber; in the south; the eastern coast; the lands about the mouth of the Po.
6. Early governments in Italy; the city of Rome.

II.—Romulus and the Beginning of Rome.

1. Difficulty of learning how and when Rome was founded; the belief of the Romans.
2. Early life of Romulus.
3. Founding of the city.
4. Seizure of the Sabine women; war; the Sabines settle at Rome.
5. The rule of Romulus.
6. His disappearance.

III.—Numa, the Peaceful King.

1. Election of Numa.
2. His character and policy
3. The Roman religion; the gods Jupiter Mars, Juno, Minerva, Vesta, and Janus.
4. The worship of the gods arranged by Numa: the Vestal Virgins; the dancing priests of Mars.
5. Death of Numa.

IV.—The Last of the Kings.

1. New wars: their lesson for the Romans; Alba Longa destroyed.

2. New walls; sewers; the temple on the Capitol.
3. The Sybilline books.
4. Tarquin the Proud, the seventh king.
5. Tarquin driven out, and a republic set up.

V.—THE WAR WITH LARS PORSENA.

1. Plot of the young nobles to restore Tarquin; the judgment of Brutus.
2. Lars Porsena aids Tarquin.
3. Horatius at the Bridge.

VI.—THE STORIES OF MUCIUS AND CLŒLIA.

1. The story of Mucius.
2. Lars Porsena makes peace.
3. The story of Clœlia.
4. The last war with Tarquin; Castor and Pollux.

VII.—SECESSION OF THE PLEBEIANS.

1. Patricians and plebeians.
2. The grievances of the plebeians.
3. Struggles between the classes.
4. The secession to the Sacred Mount.
5. Tribunes appointed to protect the plebeians.
6. Continued struggles.

VIII.—THE STORY OF CORIOLANUS.

1. Early life of Caius Marcius.
2. How he gained the name Coriolanus.
3. His struggle with the plebeians; he is sent into exile.
4. He leads the Volscians against Rome.
5. Rome saved by Veturia.

IX.—THE FAMILY OF THE FABII.

1. Roman families.
2. The Fabii and the plebeians.
3. The Fabii march against the Veientians.
4. Destruction of the Fabii.

X.—The Victory of Cincinnatus.

1. The wars with the Æquians.
2. A Roman army entrapped.
3. Cincinnatus made Dictator.
4. His victory over the Æquians.
5. Cincinnatus lays down his power.

XI.—The Laws of the Twelve Tables.

1. The early Roman law; grievances of the people.
2. Struggle to have the laws made public.
3. The "Ten Men" chosen.
4. The Twelve Tables published.
5. Their provisions.
6. Growth of the Roman law; its influence.

XII.—How Camillus Captured Veii.

1. Rome's wars with Veii; the long siege.
2. The Alban lake and the oracle of Apollo.
3. Draining the Alban lake.
4. Camillus captures Veii.
5. Removal of the gods to Rome.
6. Camillus and the treacherous schoolmaster.
7. Camillus quarrels with the people; his exile.

XIII.—The Coming of the Gauls.

1. The home of the Gauls.
2. Their appearance and manner of fighting.
3. Settlement of the Gauls in northern Italy.
4. The Gauls before Clusium; action of the Roman ambassadors.
5. The Gauls march upon Rome.
6. The battle; defeat and flight of the Romans.

XIV.—The Gauls in Rome.

1. Dismay in the city; the Roman plans.
2. The Gauls enter Rome; the old men in the Forum.
3. Slaughter of the old men; burning of the city.
4. Siege of the Capitol.

5. Camillus's victory over a band of the Gauls; the messenger to the Senate.
6. The attempt of the Gauls to surprise the Capitol; its failure.
7. The Gauls agree to depart from Rome; their terms.

XV.—Rebuilding the City.

1. Despair of the people; proposal to remove to Veii.
2. Speech of Camillus.
3. Decision to remain at Rome.
4. Rebuilding the city.
5. Wars with the neighboring peoples; victories of Camillus.
6. The last war of Camillus; his noble spirit.
7. Death of Camillus; his services to Rome.

XVI.—The New Rome

1. Recovery of Rome from her misfortunes.
2. End of the struggle between the plebeians and patricians.
3. The building of aqueducts.
4. Roman roads; the Appian Way.
5. What Rome learned from other nations.
6. Devotion of the Romans to their city: the story of Marcus Curtius; the sacrifice of Decius Mus.

XVII.—The War with Pyrrhus.

1. The Greeks of Southern Italy.
2. Rome's quarrel with Tarentum.
3. Tarentum calls in King Pyrrhus.
4. The first battle with Pyrrhus; the Roman and the Greek modes of fighting; defeat of the Romans.
5. Embassy of Cinias to Rome; speech of Appius Claudius.
6. Fabricius and Pyrrhus.
7. Second battle with Pyrrhus; the Romans again defeated.
8. Pyrrhus in Sicily.
9. The third battle; victory of the Romans; Pyrrhus leaves Italy.
10. Capture of Tarentum; Rome the ruler of the peninsula.

XVIII.—ROME AND THE CARTHAGINIANS.

1. The Carthaginians: their mother-country; their voyages; their inventions; the city of Carthage.
2. Rivalry with Rome in Sicily; beginning of the first war.
3. Strength of the two peoples.
4. The Romans build a fleet; the "crows"; Roman victories.
5. Regulus in Africa; his capture.
6. Embassy of Regulus to Rome; his death.
7. Length of the war; Roman misfortunes.
8. The Romans build a new fleet; its victory.
9. The treaty of peace.

XIX.—THE WAR WITH HANNIBAL.

1. Civil war at Carthage; Hamilcar.
2. Hamilcar goes to Spain; the oath of Hannibal.
3. Carthage conquers Spain; Hannibal becomes commander of the army.
4. Beginning of the second war between Rome and Carthage.
5. Hannibal's plans.
6. His march across the Alps.
7. Arrival in Italy; his successes.
8. Roman fear of Hannibal.
9. Causes of Hannibal's failure; his recall.
10. Scipio Africanus; defeat of Hannibal at Zama.
11. Terms of peace.
12. Last years of Hannibal; his death.

XX.—ROME CONQUERS THE WORLD.

1. Rome's gains from Carthage.
2. Conquest of Northern Italy and Southern Gaul.
3. Conquest of Macedonia.
4. The Romans in Asia Minor and in Egypt.
5. The third war with Carthage; destruction of the city; Roman power in Africa.
6. Good results of Roman rule.
7. Effects of the conquests on the Roman generals; on the common soldiers.

8. Æmilius Paullus: his reforms; his victories over Macedonia; his just dealings.
9. The triumph of Æmilius.

XXI.—THE GRACCHI AND THEIR MOTHER.

1. Roman marriage customs.
2. Marriage of Tiberius Gracchus and Cornelia, daughter of Scipio Africanus; death of Gracchus; Cornelia and her children.
3. Young Tiberius Gracchus; his service in the army.
4. Troubles of the Roman farmers; slavery; decay of the people.
5. Tiberius Gracchus elected tribune; he attempts to cure these evils.
6. Mistakes of Tiberius; he is put to death; character of the new party struggles at Rome.
7. Caius Gracchus; his election as tribune; his reforms; his death.
8. Conduct of Cornelia.

XXII.—THE WARS OF CAIUS MARIUS.

1. Caius Marius; the eagle's nest; the saying of Scipio Æmilianus.
2. Marius and the war against Jugurtha; his first consulship.
3. The invasion of the Germans.
4. Victories of Marius over the Germans.
5. Marius's sixth consulship; his failure as a statesman.
6. Civil war between the parties of Marius and Sulla.
7. The victories of Sulla; wanderings of Marius; departure of Sulla.
8. Return of Marius to Rome; his cruelties; his seventh consulship and death.
9. Return of Sulla; his terrible vengeance; sufferings of Italy.

XXIII.—CICERO, THE ORATOR.

1. Birth of Cicero; his home life and training.
2. Roman schools; Cicero's life till he was fifteen.
3. Cicero in the law-courts.
4. His first case; his fear of Sulla's anger; travels in Greece.
5. Cicero enters politics; trial of Verres.

6. His election as consul; Catiline's conspiracy.
7. Evils of Roman government; Cicero's plans.
8. New civil wars; Cicero's course.
9. Cicero's death; his character.

XXIV.—Julius Cæsar, the Conqueror of Gaul.

1. Cæsar's youth; Sulla wishes to put him to death.
2. Cæsar in the East; his first training in war.
3. His adventure with the pirates.
4. Cæsar at Rome; his habits.
5. Cæsar made overseer of the public games.
6. Character of the games: the chariot races; the wild beast hunts; the gladiatorial combats.
7. Cæsar and Pompey; Cæsar elected consul, and made governor of Gaul.
8. Condition of Gaul.
9. Cæsar's victory over the Swiss.
10. His march against the Germans; trouble with his soldiers.
11. Extent of his conquests; expeditions into Germany and Britain.
12. Cæsar's character as a general.

XXV.—Cæsar and the Beginning of the Empire.

1. Failure of the government of Rome; the remedy.
2. Pompey joins the party of the Senate; plans against Cæsar.
3. Cæsar crosses the Rubicon; the second civil war begins.
4. Flight of Pompey to Greece; Cæsar goes to Spain.
5. Cæsar follows Pompey to Greece; defeat and death of Pompey.
6. Further conquests of Cæsar; mutiny of his soldiers.
7. Cæsar's four-fold triumph.
8. Cæsar as Emperor; his reforms.
9. Plot against Cæsar; his death.
10. His character.

XXVI.—Rome in the Time of Augustus.

1. Struggles after Cæsar's death; his nephew becomes Emperor.
2. The good rule of Augustus; boundaries of the Empire.
3. Literature under Augustus; the poet Horace.

4. A day in Rome: clients and the morning reception; the business in the Forum; the mid-day rest; exercise in the Field of Mars; the baths; the banquet.

XXVII.—The Empire after Augustus.

1. The successors of Augustus; Nero.
2. The Good Emperors: Trajan; Hadrian; Marcus Aurelius.
3. Decline of the Empire; danger from the Germans; the emperor Diocletian.
4. Constantine the Great; the Christian religion; Constantinople.
5. Division of the Empire; attacks of the Germans; fall of the Empire of the West.
6. The German conquest paves the way for modern Europe.

XXVIII.—The Christians and the Empire.

1. Spread of Christianity in the Empire.
2. Attitude of the government; "To the lions with the Christians!"
3. Persecution under Nero.
4. The Catacombs.
5. Bravery of the Martyrs; Polycarp.
6. Failure of the persecutions to check the growth of Christianity.
7. The Empire becomes Christian; Constantine; end of the old religion.

XXIX.—The Remains of Rome.

1. Roman remains: language, laws, ruins.
2. Eruption of Vesuvius, 79 A. D.
3. Discovery of the buried cities; Pompeii.
4. Streets and public buildings of Pompeii.
5. The private dwellings.
6. Pictures and furniture.
7. Pompeiian shops.
8. Writings on the walls.
9. Disappearance of the ancient remains at Rome.
10. The old in the new.

CHRONOLOGICAL OUTLINE.

For the sake of completeness, some names and events have been introduced into this outline which are not mentioned in the text. These are distinguished by being printed in *italics*.

B.C.

753. Rome founded (legendary date).

753–509. **Rome under the rule of Kings:** Romulus, Numa *Pompilius, Tullus Hostilius, Ancus Marcius, Tarquinius Priscus, Servius Tullius, Tarquinius Superbus* (Tarquin the Proud).

509. The Kings driven out, and a **republic set up.**

509–345. Frequent **wars** with the Etruscans, Volscians, Æquians, and other neighboring peoples. Struggle for existence during the first sixty years; after that, neighboring country gradually conquered.

494. **Secession of the plebeians** to the Sacred Mount. Creation of the **tribunes of the people.**

451. Ten men (*Decemvirs*) appointed to rule the state and publish the laws; the **Twelve Tables of the Law.** (*Misrule of Appius Claudius; the story of Virginia.*)

396. Capture of Veii by Camillus.

390. Battle by the brook *Allia*, and **capture of Rome by the Gauls.**

367. **Plebeians admitted to the consulship,** (*laws of Licinius and Sextius*).

343–290. *Three wars with the Samnites* (*a mountain people of Southern Italy*). *Revolt and conquest of the Latin neighbors of Rome. The Romans become the chief people in Italy.*

282–272. **War with King Pyrrhus;** battles of *Heraclea, Ausculum,* and *Beneventum;* conquest of Tarentum. Rome now mistress of the peninsula of Italy.

264–241. First War with Carthage. Rome gains Sicily and (later) *Sardinia.*

225–222. Cis-Alpine Gaul (the valley of the Po) conquered.

218–201. Second War with Carthage. Hannibal marches into Italy; battles of *Ticinus, Trebia, and Lake Trasimenus;* battle of *Cannae;* Roman victories in Spain and Sicily; Hannibal's reinforcements defeated in the battle of the *Metaurus;* Roman victories in Africa; recall of Hannibal; battle of Zama.

200–168. Wars with Macedonia. Battle of *Cynoscephalæ; Greek states set free from Macedonia;* victory of Æmilius Paullus over King Perseus at *Pydna.* (Macedonia made a Roman province, 146 B.C.)

192–189. *War with Syria* (in Asia).

149–146. Third War with Carthage. Capture and destruction of the city by *Scipio Æmilianus.*

146. *War with Greek states (Achæan league). Destruction of Corinth.*

143–133. *Wars with the tribes of Spain.*

133. **Tiberius Gracchus** elected tribune.

123. **Caius Gracchus** elected tribune.

111–105. War with Jugurtha, in Africa.

113–101. Wars with German tribes (*Cimbri and Teutones*). Victories of Marius at *Aquæ Sextiæ* (102), and *Vercellæ* (101).

90–88. *Revolt of the Italians: Rome forced to admit them to citizenship.*

88–64. *Three wars with King Mithradates of Pontus* (*in Asia Minor*). The first war was brought to an end by Sulla; the third by Pompey, by whom Pontus was annexed to the Roman territory.

88–82. Civil war between Sulla (party of the nobles) **and Marius** (party of the people).

80–72. *Rebellion in Spain (under Sertorius);* put down by Pompey.

73–71. Rebellion of gladiators and slaves about Mt. Vesuvius (under *Spartacus*); put down by Pompey.

67. Pompey overcomes the pirates.

66–62. Plot of Catiline at Rome; **Cicero** consul.

60. Agreement between Pompey, Cæsar, and Crassus (*first triumvirate*). **Cæsar elected consul.**

58–51. Conquest of Gaul by Cæsar.

49–48. **Civil war between Cæsar and Pompey.** Defeat of Pompey at *Pharsalus.* Cæsar becomes sole ruler of Rome (emperor).

48–45. War against the followers of Pompey in Africa and Spain.

44, March 15. Cæsar slain. (Brutus and *Cassius*, leaders of the plot.)

42. Brutus and Cassius defeated by Octavius (the nephew of Cæsar) and *Antony*, in the *battle of Philippi.*

31–30. War between Octavius and *Antony. Defeat of Antony at Actium.* Octavius becomes Emperor, and takes the name Augustus.

31 B.C. }
14 A.D. } **Augustus,** emperor.

54–68. Nero, emperor. Fire at Rome; persecution of the Christians.

98–117. Trajan, emperor.

117–138. Hadrian, emperor.

161–180. Marcus Aurelius, emperor.

284–305. Diocletian, emperor.

323–337. **Constantine the Great.** The empire becones Christian; founding of Constantinople as the capital of the empire.

375. The **German tribes** begin to come into the Empire in large numbers.

395. The Empire permanently divided into a Western Empire, with its capital at Rome, and an Eastern Empire, with its capital at Constantinople.

410. Rome plundered by the *Goths* under *Alaric.*

476. **End of the Western Empire.**

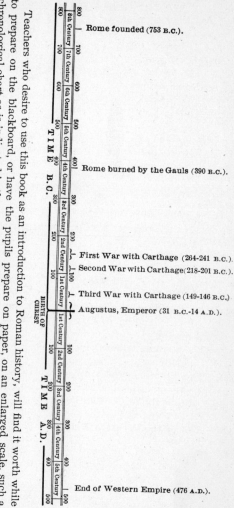

Rome founded (753 B.C.).

Rome burned by the Gauls (390 B.C.).

First War with Carthage (264-241 B.C.).
Second War with Carthage (218-201 B.C.).

Third War with Carthage (149-146 B.C.)
Augustus, Emperor (31 B.C.-14 A.D.).

End of Western Empire (476 A.D.).

Teachers who desire to use this book as an introduction to Roman history, will find it worth while to prepare on the blackboard, or have the pupils prepare on paper, on an enlarged scale, such a chronological chart as is indicated in the accompanying cut. If the latter plan is adopted, strips of paper four or five feet long by seven or eight inches broad should be used; if these are not readily obtainable, a half-dozen sheets of letter-paper, pasted together end to end, will answer. By writing on *both* sides of the central lines, space may be found for putting in all the more important events of Roman history. The chart may be made manageable by rolling it, or better, perhaps, by folding it (alternately over and back, after the fashion of a set of panoramic photographic views) on the lines separating the century divisions.

OFFICERS UNDER THE REPUBLIC.

1. **Consuls, two:** Elected for one year, and acted as heads of the state, and commanders of the army. Patricians only could be chosen, at first; after 367 B. C. both might be, and one must be, Plebeian.

2. **Dictator, one:** Appointed in time of danger or for a special purpose; could hold office for six months, but usually resigned before that, as soon as the work was done. The Dictator held the highest power in the state, the consul and all other officers being under his orders. He usually appointed a "Master of the Horse" as his second in command.

3. **Tribunes, ten:** Established 494 B. C. Elected for one year; must be Plebeians; had the right to "veto" any proceeding; their persons were sacred.

4. **Other Officers:** Two **Censors,** elected every fifth year, to take a census of the people, and revise the lists of the Senate, the tribes, etc. Four **Ædiles,** who kept order in the city, and had charge of the public buildings and markets; two of these, called *curule ædiles*, also had charge of the games and gladiatorial shows. One or more **Prætors,** who acted as judges at Rome, and served as governors of the provinces.

ASSEMBLIES.

I. ASSEMBLIES OF THE PEOPLE.

1. **Assembly of the People by Curies,** or groups of families. This was made up only of Patricians, and soon lost its power in the state.

2. **Assembly of the People by Centuries.** Servius Tullius divided all of the free Romans, both Patricians and Plebeians, into groups or centuries, according to their wealth. In the assembly of the Centuries, the vote was taken by these groups, so that

Plebeians and Patricians both voted in this body. The power in the state gradually passed from the assembly of the Curies to this new assembly, and it came to be the body which made laws, elected officers, declared war, and concluded peace.

3. **Assembly of the People by Tribes.** Besides being divided into classes by their wealth, the Romans were also divided into twenty-six tribes, according to their places of residence. In the assembly of the Tribes, the Plebeians alone took part at first, and the assembly had little power beyond electing the Tribunes. Gradually the Patricians were admitted to it, and it increased in importance till it could make laws which were binding on both Patricians and Plebeians. It ended by becoming the most important of the assemblies of the people.

II. THE SENATE.

This body was composed of the chief men of Rome, especially those who had filled the offices of Consul, Prætor, and the like. Vacancies were filled up by the Censors, who also had power to expel unworthy members. Under the Republic, there were three hundred Senators, at first, but the number was afterward increased. The Senate watched over the government, and advised both the people and the officers of the state. It came to be the most powerful body in Rome, but from time to time the people asserted their power against it.

INDEX.